Brooklyn's Neighborhoods

0   1   2

MILES

USHWICK

CYPRESS HILLS

venue

QUEENS

NEW LOTS

EAST NEW YORK

ROWNS-
VILLE

CANARSIE

ILL
ASIN

GATEWAY NATIONAL RECREATION AREA

Jamaica Bay

THE ROCKAWAYS

ATLANTIC OCEAN

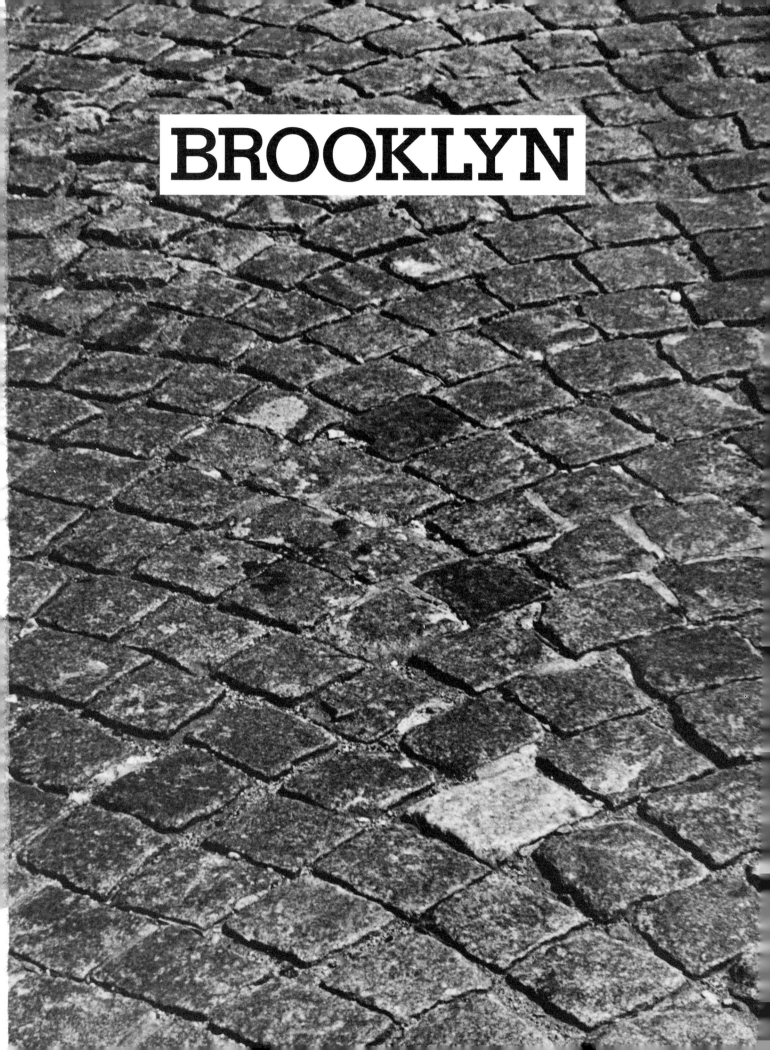

BROOKLYN

BROOKLYN

...AND HOW IT GOT THAT WAY

BY DAVID W. McCULLOUGH
PHOTOGRAPHS BY JIM KALETT

THE DIAL PRESS
NEW YORK

PUBLISHED BY
The Dial Press
1 Dag Hammarskjold Plaza
New York, New York 10017

Grateful acknowledgment is made
to the following for permission to reprint
previously published material:

Jewel Music Publishing Co., Inc.: From "Leave Us Go Root
for the Dodgers, Rodgers," words and music by Ted Berkman,
Dan Parker, and Bud Green. Copyright © 1942, renewed
Jewel Music Publishing Co., Inc., New York, N.Y.

Liveright Publishing Corporation: From *The Bridge*, by
Hart Crane. Copyright 1933, © 1958, 1970 by Liveright
Publishing Corporation.

The New York Times Company: From "Pope, in Farewell,
Tells New Yorkers 'A City Needs a Soul,'" October 1979.
Copyright © 1979 by The New York Times Company.

Random House, Inc.: From "Local Color" in *The Dogs Bark:
Public People and Private Places*, by Truman Capote.
Copyright © 1973 by Truman Capote.

Charles Scribner's Sons: From "Only the Dead Know
Brooklyn" (copyright 1935 F-R Publishing Corp., copyright
renewed 1963 Paul Gitlin) in *From Death to Morning*, by
Thomas Wolfe. Copyright 1935 Charles Scribner's Sons;
copyright renewed 1963 Paul Gitlin.

Viking Penguin Inc.: From "The Camperdown Elm" in
The Complete Poems of Marianne Moore. Copyright © 1967
by Marianne Moore. Originally published in *The New
Yorker*. From "Hometown Piece for Messrs. Alston and
Reese" in *The Complete Poems of Marianne Moore*.
Copyright © 1959 by Marianne Moore.

Design by Holly McNeely
Endpaper maps by David Lindroth

Library of Congress Cataloging in Publication Data

McCullough, David W.
Brooklyn—and how it got that way.

Bibliography: p. 269

Includes index.
1. Brooklyn (New York, N.Y.)—History. 2. Brooklyn
(New York, N.Y.)—Description. 3. Brooklyn (New York,
N.Y.)—Social life and customs. 4. New York (N.Y.)—
History. 5. New York (N.Y.)—Description. 6. New York
(N.Y.)—Social life and customs. I. Kalett, Jim. II. Title.
F129.B7M33   1983   974.7'23   82-13731
ISBN 0-385-27427-0
First edition

For Fran, whose letters were postmarked Brooklyn

AUTHOR'S
ACKNOWLEDGMENTS

To write about Brooklyn and be named McCullough probably requires some sort of clarification. I am not one of the Coney Island McCulloughs, the Tilyou in-laws who introduced the Island's first moving targets in their shooting gallery off Surf Avenue and whose merry-go-round, now restored and operating next to the Prospect Park Zoo, has remained one of the borough's longest-running delights. And although we share the same first and last names I'm not related to the David McCullough whose *The Great Bridge* is a work of engineering and social history as impressive and provocative as its subject, the Brooklyn Bridge.

I have, though, lived in Brooklyn as an adult for seventeen years, and while there is some truth to the adage that people in Brooklyn know only the parts of town that lie between their neighborhood and Manhattan, it is also true that Brooklyn, more than most cities I know, inspires long walks. The title Alfred Kazin chose for his memoirs of growing up in Brownsville is an apt one. It is difficult to live in Brooklyn and not become a walker in the city. This book would never have been written if it had not been for those seventeen years, spent in three different neighborhoods, and for the walks that took place over those years, first alone, then with friends, then with my wife Frances, and finally with our children, Ben and Katy.

The book would also have been impossible without libraries, the libraries of the Long Island Historical Society and the New-York Historical Society, the New York Public Library, the Brooklyn Public Library (two different organizations: the cities of New York and Brooklyn may have become one in 1898, but their books never did), the Library of Congress, and the Hastings-on-Hudson Public Library.

Perhaps most important of all are the people who helped. They include: Jeanette Hopkins (who allowed me to read the manuscript of her father Carleton Hopkins' memoirs of growing up in Park Slope and Bedford-Stuyvesant at the turn of the century); Clifton Fadiman; Frank Scioscia; Anne Jackson; Jody Zakrevsky of the New York City Department of Parks and Recreation; Marcy Protter; Norma Marshall; Morris Weisenthal; Joseph Landau and Nanette Rainone of the Brooklyn Borough President's Office; Jack Mahon, Robert Massa and Richard Aneiro of the Brooklyn Navy Yard Development Corporation; Mary Idoni; Lucy Vocola; Jack Goodman of *Ring* magazine; Olly Carey, Tom McGreal, Walter De Sheers, and Salvatore W. Notarile of the New York Dock Railway; staff members of the National Park Service Gateway Center; Elizabeth White of the Brooklyn Public Library; John Manbeck of the Kingsboro Historical Society; Arthur J. Konop of the James A. Kelly Institute for Local Historical Studies at St. Francis College; and Russell Bastedo, formerly of the Long Island Historical Society.

Finally I would like to mention a group of people who, separately, by being in the right place at different times helped bring this book into being: Curt Bruce, Susan Ann Protter, Michael George, Larry Michelotti, and Rick Kot.

In "Crossing Brooklyn Ferry" Walt Whitman asked, "What is it then between us?" and, as was his custom, offered an exuberant catalogue of answers. Among them was "I too lived, Brooklyn of ample hills was mine." For these acknowledgments I'll change that "mine" to "ours."

D. W. McC.

PHOTOGRAPHER'S ACKNOWLEDGMENTS

I am indebted to numerous people who gave assistance in one way or another, through city agencies, as members of block associations, churches, and as individuals I met spontaneously on location who gave advice or just good directions. There isn't space to mention all the names, nor do I know them all, but their help has enriched the book.

There are those who went far out of their way to provide me with access and information whom I would like to mention by name. Cooperation that came from the Office of the Borough President, Howard Golden, President, was surprisingly non-political. The people there are devoted to Brooklyn and I want to thank Jill Kelly, Joe Landau, and Gail Hammerman for being indispensable. At the Port Authority of New York and New Jersey, I am grateful to Jim Malone and especially Jane Reilly for helicopters, piers, and enthusiasm.

I thank also Tupper Thomas, Administrator of Prospect Park and her assistant, Paul Berizzi; the New York City Police Department, Brooklyn South Task Force, Chief Robert Johnston; New York City Fire Department; New York City Department of Sanitation; Brooklyn Navy Yard Development Corporation, Richard J. Aneiro, President, David Lenefsky, Chairman of the Board; City of New York, Community Planning Board #3, William P. Irish,

Chairman, Priscilla Boyles, District Manager; Williamsburgh Savings Bank, James E. Dawson, Assistant Vice-President; Universal Maritime Service Corp., Mr. James G. Costello, President.

The following individuals were most enthusiastic and helpful: Father Joseph Nugent, Monsignor James Hunt, and Ruth Mitchell in Bed-Stuy; Paul Ursini in Bensonhurst; Bruce LaRoche and Ozzie Brown of the Muslim Community in Bushwick; Marilyn Bigman in Greenpoint; Phil Manna in Williamsburg; Rabbi Jacob Bronner from Boro Park; Wendy Weller, Chairwoman, Flatbush Development Corporation; A. Robert Koenig, Superintendent, Greenwood Cemetery.

Finally, four people were most important: Phillip A. Harrington, photographer and friend, for photo editing and good criticism; Bob Kapstatter, Brooklyn Editor of the New York *Daily News*, for suggestions, arrangements, and constant interest; David W. McCullough, a long-time friend, for his faith in my work; and Carolyn, my wife, for driving me hundreds of miles over the Borough, editing down all the contact sheets and being my eyes.

J.K.

"I want to go to Brooklyn."
—**William Makepeace Thackeray, 1852**

"Brooklyn happens to be one of those things that can expand. The more you put into it, the more it will hold."
—**Brooklyn Monthly, 1869**

"It'd take a guy a lifetime to know Brooklyn t'roo an' t'roo. An' even den, yuh wouldn't know it all."
—**Thomas Wolfe, 1935**

"Terribly funny, yes, but Brooklyn is also a sad brutal provincial lonesome human silent sprawling raucous lost passionate subtle bitter immature innocent perverse tender mysterious place, a place where Crane and Whitman found poems, a mythical dominion against whose shores the Coney Island sea laps a wintry lament."
—**Truman Capote, 1946**

"John Paul lingered over the small details of his goodbye at Shea Stadium. He evoked partisan roars as he saluted the parts of the metropolis with slow, deep-voiced care: 'Long Island, New Jersey, Connecticut. And Brooklyn.' His pronunciation of the latter—'Broke-leen'— was savored by the crowd, and they responded with their biggest roar of outer-borough, suburbanite approval. . . . 'Brooklyn. It is my second visit to Brooklyn— the second in my life.' "
—**The New York Times, 1979**

CONTENTS

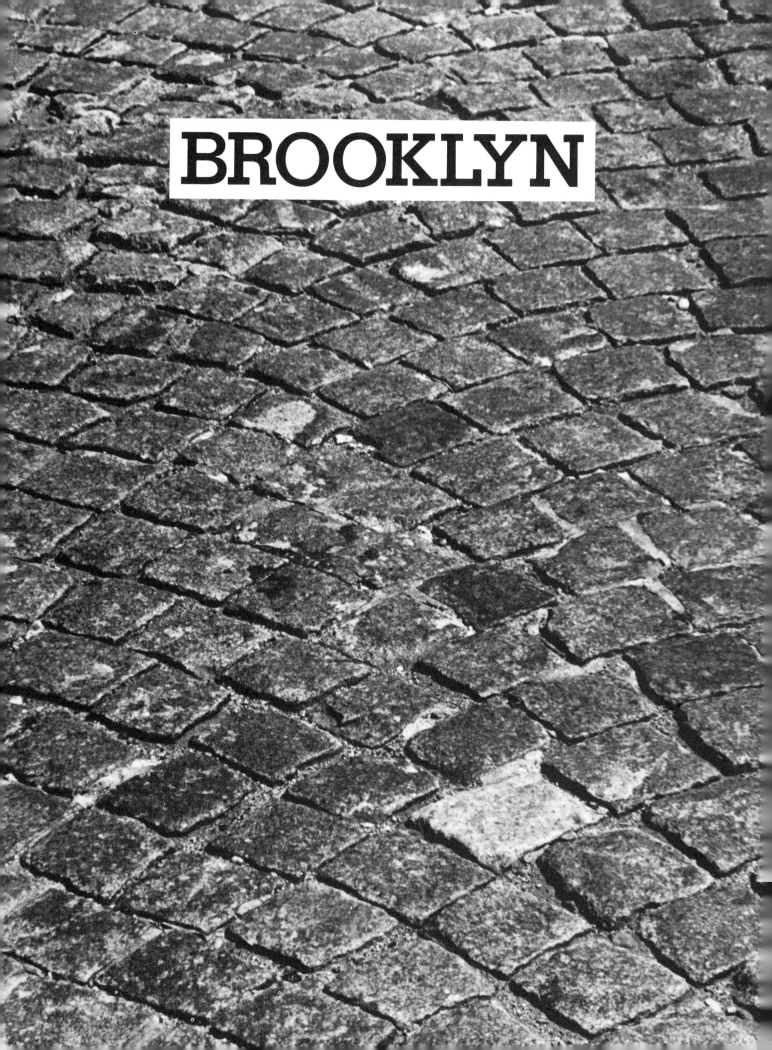

BROOKLYN

CHAPTER ONE
A City of Growing Villages

The Ice Age may have ended in Brooklyn. Nearly a million years ago the forward edge of the great glacier slid over Long Island, ground to a halt, sat for several hundred thousand years, melted a bit, and then slowly retreated northward. On the sandy flatland of the western end of the island it left behind rubble dragged from the mainland, rocky heaps and ridges that in time grew over with underbrush and trees and took on the place names that were to give the area its particular character: Brooklyn Heights, Cobble Hill, Park Slope, Bay Ridge, Crow Hill, Mount Prospect, Cypress Hills. The name Brooklyn itself, from the Dutch *Breukelen*, meant "broken valley."

These names, of course, were gifts of white settlers and land developers, who began arriving in the early seventeenth century. The Indian inhabitants, the Canarsees, simply called Brooklyn the Sandy Place and let it go at that. A branch of the Lenni-Lenape that had established a dozen or so semipermanent villages scattered across Brooklyn, the Canarsees lived a quiet life kept tranquil largely through annual payments to the more warlike Mohawks to the north. The tribe had no supreme chief in peacetime but many local clan leaders. They were matriarchal: grandmothers and great-aunts directed family activities, and men lived in their wives' households. Their farming lands were located near inland villages, but in the late spring, after the corn was planted, the clans moved to the seashore, present-day Coney Island, where they dug oysters and clams, both for food and for the shells, which were worked into the wampum tribute money for the Mohawks.

The first Dutch contact with the area was when Henry Hudson's *Half-Moon*, under contract to the Dutch East India Company, sailed into New York Harbor in 1609. With the ship anchored off Coney Island, a scouting party of Hudson's men met some deerskin-clad Indians (described as "very civil"), who were invited aboard to trade green tobacco for knives and beads. The Indians also brought maize, corn bread, and hemp with them. One of Hudson's men wrote that the shoreline was "full of great tall oaks, and the lands were pleasant with grass and flowers and goodly trees . . . and very sweet smells came from them." The story ends sadly with a sailor named John Colman being shot in the neck by an arrow and later buried on the beach. This may have happened at Coney Island, although Sandy Hook, New Jersey, also claims the honor of being the site of the first white man's grave on the New York waterfront.

Hudson promptly kidnapped two Indians, not in revenge for Colman's death, he said, but simply as souvenirs, mementos of the voyage to take back to the stockholders in Holland. The *Half-Moon* then sailed up the river that was to bear Hudson's name, passing Manhattan Island and not stopping until it reached the future site of Albany. Here the river was only seven feet deep, and Hudson decided that it was probably not going to take him to the Orient after all. He turned his little ship around, headed south again, and passed through the Narrows to the open sea on October 4, thirty-two days after he had entered the harbor. As for the kidnapped Indians, those early Brooklynites, they never reached Holland. They jumped ship somewhere upriver and organized the local tribes in a none-too-successful ambush of the *Half-Moon*, probably at the narrow bend in the river where the Bear Mountain Bridge stands today.

For the next ten years or so various Dutch trading schemes came into and went out of existence. Upstate Indians traded valuable beaver pelts to Europeans, who had no desire—or reason, for that matter—to set up permanent settlements. Western Long Island, which lacked the furry wealth of the river valley, was ignored. But in 1621 a mammoth monopoly was established, the

Dutch West India Company, which was to control all Dutch activity in North and South America, the West Indies, and even parts of Africa. The American lands were named New Netherlands. A New Amsterdam was built on the tip of Manhattan. Tiny farming villages were laid out on the Gowanus Creek in Breukelen and out on the flatlands of Jamaica Bay, where salty sea grasses could be harvested for cattle. Fortified farmhouses sprung up on Newtown Creek, the current boundary with Queens, and on Wallabout Bay, which later became the Navy Yard.

The Canarsees and the Dutch colonists shared a common weakness: they both dabbled in real estate and set great store in elegantly phrased bills of sale. Beginning in 1636, when settlers began buying up land on a section of Jamaica Bay they first called Nieuw Amersfoort (Peter Stuyvesant preferred to call the area the Flats, and the name Flatlands stuck), a series of impressive legal documents formalized the transactions. For Barren Islands —which nearly three centuries later joined Brooklyn proper through the magic of landfill—Wawmatt Tappa and Kack-a-washke received "two coats, one kettel, one new trooper-coat, ten fathoms of wampum prage, three shirts, six pounds of powder, six bars of lead and a quantity of Brandie wine." They were also promised "one-half of all such whale-fish that shall by winds and storms be cast upon the said Island."

Through hundreds of such agreements the Dutch pieced together six towns by 1660: Flatlands, t'Vlache Bos (Flatbush, the wooded plain), Boswijk (Bushwick, the town of woods), Gravesend (for either the town in England or 's Gravensande, Dutch for the count's beach), and Nieuw Utrecht and Breukelen (both named for towns back in Holland). Over the next two hundred years the villages would grow and join together to become the City of Brooklyn.

Oddly enough, though all but one of these villages were located on the water, the settlers ignored the ocean, the bay, and the river. They were by habit farmers, not fishermen or sailors, and except for a handful of men in Breukelen who worked the ferry and a few Gowanus oystermen and beachcombers who picked over the shore in search of quahog and periwinkle shells that could be turned into negotiable wampum, the early Brooklynites turned their backs to the sea.

In his history of New York City the young Teddy Roosevelt criticized these farmers for lacking the true pioneer spirit, a spirit he seemed to associate with chopping down trees. "The Dutch settlers," he wrote, "took slowly and with reluctance to that all-important tool and weapon of the American pioneer, the axe, and chopped down very little timber indeed." Actually, at rocky, wooded Flatbush, the only inland settlement, the Dutch did clear the land (although they didn't fence in their cattle, which caused some squabbles with the Indians) and later even took advantage of the breezy highlands to build a few windmills.

The Dutch West India Company controlled all aspects of the settlers' lives, and it controlled them for a single purpose: to make money for the stockholders. In other bays and inlets along the Atlantic Coast other colonies were established for religious or social reasons or simply for the personal profit of the settlers themselves. In the Dutch settlements the only ideology was the question of profit or loss for the investors back home. Some governors, such as Peter Stuyvesant, equated fiscal prudence with strict moral law. But that was their own policy, not the company's. When a Dutch governor tried expelling Jews from New Amsterdam, he was reprimanded by the company, which stated that "the conscience of men ought to be free and unshackled." But this was not a moral decision. The company needed settlers in New Netherlands, and if it couldn't get proper Calvinists, it would take what it could get.

To lure "Christian people of tender conscience" to North America, the company took to advertising in newspapers. A notice that ran in London promised "the best clymate in the whole world [where] seed may be thrown into the ground, except six weekes, the yere long; there are five sorts of grape wch are very good and grow heere naturally . . . ; heere growth tobacco very good, it naturally abounds . . . furrs of all sorts may bee had of the natives very reasonable . . . ; marvelous plenty in all kinds of food . . . ; the sea and rivers abounding with excellent fat and wholesome fish wch are heere in great plenty."

Tobacco did grow at Greenpoint along the East River, and grapes flourished on Brooklyn trellises, but the best climate in the whole world also included some hellish winters, and the "natives" could become quite unreasonable. Dominie Megapolensis, the pastor who founded the Dutch Reformed churches in Flatlands and

New Utrecht Reformed Church, built in 1828

Flatbush, wrote to a friend back home that the dangerous snakes had rattles on their tails to warn the unwary, that there were plenty of furs available to keep off the cold winds, and that if at one moment "the clouds will appear as if they would spew cats," an hour later there would not be a cloud in the sky. These were hardly major inducements to a prospective Dutch settler who could choose among the rich forests of northern Brazil, the warm sands of Curaçao, and the lucrative slave markets of Angola.

It is hardly a surprise that most of Brooklyn's six villages grew slowly. From the beginning Breukelen—directly across the East River from New Amsterdam—had commercial potential, and Flatbush was always a busy country market town. The rest remained isolated settlements of a few farmhouses—usually long, low buildings with heavy overhanging roofs—protected by a wooden stockade. The farmlands were outside of town, and the best of them were long strips that took advantage of the changing topography, from the sweet sea grass along the water to the flatlands for pasture to the inland forests with their valuable woodlots.

The stockades were for protection against the Indians. Years later, in the 1890s, when a group of prosperous Park Slope gentlemen formed the Montauk Club and built a handsome clubhouse vaguely suggested by the Ca' d'Oro in Venice, they decorated the exterior not with Italianate cherubs but with thoroughly American eagles and scenes of local Indian life. One frieze runs around three sides of the building, and according to the novelist L. J. Davis, it depicts—depending on which end of the building you begin to view it from—either a war ending with a peace treaty or a peace treaty followed by a war. That ambiguity nicely sums up the Indian situation in the mid-seventeenth century in Brooklyn. There was no lack of treaties and bills of sale. What they meant, however, was debatable.

The Dutch claimed that since the agreements were with them, the Canarsees no longer had to pay tribute to the Mohawks, and under the orders of Governor Willem Kieft the Dutch began to take the valuable gifts for themselves. In 1643 Kieft seized two wagonloads of corn, killing several Indians in the process. The result, interrupted by a peace treaty or two, was Kieft's War.

Marauding Mohawks destroyed farmhouses along Newtown

Creek. The Bennett place on the Gowanus, one of the first houses in Breukelen, was burned. Gravesend was attacked, and the settlers had to flee to Flatlands. The war spread as far as Westchester, where the religious leader Anne Hutchinson and her family were killed. It all ended with a company of fifty men from New Amsterdam massacring nearly five hundred Indians at Horse Neck, near Greenwich, Connecticut.

But that was pretty much the last time that anyone in Brooklyn was bothered by, or even much noticed, the Indians. A local law passed in 1655 said that no Indian "could pow wow or perform worship to the devil" within the limits of any town in the colony, but it wasn't needed in Brooklyn. The Indians were on their way to becoming harmless town characters. As one nineteenth-century clergyman piously phrased it, noting the passing of what he believed to be the last of the Canarsees: "The white race grew stronger, and the Indian weaker until about 1830 when *Jim de Wilt*, or 'Jim the wildman,' died in his wretched hut . . . the miserable remnant of the once proud possessors of these fertile lands."

Old Indian trails were used by the settlers, and in time they were widened and paved to become Kings Highway and Flatbush Avenue. The Mohawks returned to the Gowanus in the 1920s, when the Manhattan skyscraper boom began, and builders found that the Indians' unusual sense of balance made them excellent workers on steel riggings hundreds of feet above the ground. Perhaps as many as a thousand settled in apartment houses and tenements not far from where the Bennett farm had burned. A few blocks away the Wigwam Bar opened its doors close to the spot where the worthy burghers of Breukelen had built their tiny Dutch Reformed church in the shape of an octagon so that it could also be used as a fort in case of Indian raids.

The Dutch Reformed churches were the center of life in all but one of the Brooklyn towns. Gravesend was the exception. In New Netherlands, Gravesend was always the exception. The town had no church and wouldn't have one until 1763. Its citizens were English-speaking, and its leader was a woman, the lady Deborah Moody, née Dunch, daughter of one of Queen Elizabeth's members of Parliament, granddaughter of the Bishop of Durham, and widow of a baronet.

One of the few surviving descriptions of Lady Moody—as she was called—refers to her as "nice and anciently religious," although a Dutch Reformed dominie from neighboring Flatlands petitioned the governor to bring charges against her for using "calumnious expressions against God's work and servants." She was probably the first woman, white woman at least, to be a political force in North America.

In 1635, as a forty-year-old English widow with two grown children, Lady Moody had been warned by the Star Chamber to start setting "a good example necessary to the poor classes." Her crime was spending too much time in London rather than staying put on the family estate in Wiltshire. She was probably also dabbling in religions outside the Church of England. Five years later she sailed for Massachusetts, became a Puritan, and bought five hundred acres in Salem. A year later she bought a house in Swampscott for eleven hundred pounds, and a year after that she was excommunicated for ostentation. (Although it was perhaps more significant that she also questioned the validity of infant baptism.) Roger Williams did not take her repeated hints that he invite her to his liberal colony in Rhode Island, so she bought a ship—money does not seem to have been one of her problems—and sailed to New Haven, where her reception was a cool one.

Perhaps there were rumors that she might come back to Massachusetts, for John Endecott wrote to John Winthrop that she must not be allowed to return unless she "acknowledge her evil in opposing the Churches, and leave her opinions behind her, for shee is a dangerous woman."

But rather than return she had "removed to the Dutch, against the advice of her friends," as Governor Winthrop noted in his journal. Accompanied by her son, Henry, she stopped first in New Amsterdam, where at Turtle Bay she met other British expatriates, including Nicholas Stillwell, "Nicholas the Tobacco Planter," as he was called in some old records. In 1643 the group won a patent for lands at Gravesend, where they planned a "city by the sea."

Planned is the key word, for unlike any other community in Brooklyn, Gravesend was a town designed to be lived in: a sixteen-acre square divided into four smaller squares of four acres each. Each of the smaller squares was divided into ten lots which surrounded a common yard, where the cattle were brought each evening. The whole complex was later surrounded by a palisade. Outside the stockade the allotted fields—forty farm lots—radiated out like spokes of a wheel. Inside, according to the plan, one section of each square would be put aside for public use: a cemetery in one, a town hall or courthouse in another, a school in the third, and a church in the fourth. The cemetery was founded and the courthouse built, the first and for many years the only one in Brooklyn. Of all the old villages Gravesend made the most lasting imprint on the map. The boundaries of the other towns have blurred or been lost, but today, with an elevated subway running right through the middle of them where McDonald Avenue crosses Gravesend Neck Road, Lady Moody's four squares, slightly off angle from the standard grid, can still be seen.

In granting a patent to Lady Moody and her followers the Dutch West India Company gave them the unheard-of right to pick their own form of government. They chose the New England town meeting system and did not elect to accept the Dutch Reformed Church. At a time when Dutch settlers could be fined fifty pounds for attending a Quaker meeting, Quakers were welcome in Gravesend, and meetings were held right in the Moody parlor. Also welcome at Gravesend was the notorious Griet Reyniers, an Amsterdam barmaid who had become New Amsterdam's first prostitute. Her husband was a mulatto named Anthony Janz van Salee, called the Turk, who claimed to have been born in Morocco, the son of a Dutch pirate who had become the sultan's admiral. Their marriage was hardly a calm one, especially when the Turk tried to reform his bride. Things came to a head when Griet threatened to smash her two daughters—"the fruits of her profession," as one historian rather primly phrased it—against a wall. She was tired of being a "nobleman's whore," she said, and intended to go back to her sailors. This was too much for the local officials, who ordered the pair out of town. They went as far as Gravesend, where they seem to have turned into a perfectly ordinary suburban couple who raised a total of four daughters and married them off to good families.

These extraordinary events at Gravesend were an affront to many serious Dutchmen. The Dominie Megapolensis reported back to officials in Amsterdam that the townspeople of Gravesend had

LEFT,
*The old cemetery
at Gravesend*
BELOW,
*Under the El in
modern Gravesend*

rejected "infant baptism, the Sabbath, the office of preacher and the teacher of God's Word saying that through these have come all sorts of contention into the world." Some Gravesenders themselves might actually have been uneasy in their freedom. In 1660, a year or perhaps two after Lady Moody's death (the date of which is uncertain), eight of them petitioned for a pastor "to end the licentious mode of living."

But there was a strong sense of law at Gravesend, as its court records bear out. Town meetings were held each month. A committee inspected the palisade fortnightly to see that it was in repair, and every man in town was required to own a twenty-foot ladder (along with a gun, a pound of gunpowder, and two pounds of lead) to be used to maintain the walls. A bounty of five guilders was paid for every wolf killed within the township. No "brandy, strong liquor or strong drink" could be sold to Indians, and only a pint of it at a time to whites. Tobacco, though, could be sold without restriction, and court records from 1647 show that one Robert Pennere was doing such a brisk business with the Indians that he had taken to stealing tobacco from his fellow colonists to keep the trade going. The most common lawsuits involved squabbles over property lines, and as late as 1789, when Aaron Burr represented Gravesend in court, there were still disagreements with Flatbush over where the town line should be drawn. While the Canarsees may have treasured their real estate bills of sale, their notion of owning land was different from that of the settlers, for to the Indians ownership simply meant the right to use the land, and not necessarily the exclusive right to use it.

There was, of course, tension between the English Gravesenders and their Dutch neighbors. Jacobus van Curler, a young teacher who lived briefly at Gravesend, left because he felt the English didn't want him and went to New Amsterdam, where he opened the town's first private school. There was some suspicion among the Dutch that the colony was allowed to exist so it could siphon off undesirables, and there may also have been some bitterness as to why the company allowed the English freedoms they themselves were denied.

A few years after Lady Moody's death open war almost broke out between Dutch and English on Coney Island. The company gave a monopoly on salt manufacture in New Netherlands to a

Dutch merchant named Dick de Wolf, who opened a saltworks out where the Gravesend pigs ran among the pumpkins. De Wolf told the local farmers to remove the livestock and stop harvesting the salt hay. The Gravesenders promptly burned down De Wolf's buildings. De Wolf protested to the council of the company, back in Holland, that Gravesend was attracting "the scum of all New England." The council ordered Peter Stuyvesant to move in with his troops and protect the saltworks. Stuyvesant, uncharacteristically, put off doing anything.

The problem solved itself in August 1664. A British ship dropped anchor in Gravesend Bay and in a few days was joined by other warships. Colonel Richard Nicholls ordered four hundred men ashore near Coney Island and sent another party across the bay to Staten Island, where they occupied a blockhouse built for protection against the Indians. Nicholls declared a blockade of New Amsterdam and called for Peter Stuyvesant to surrender the port. Stuyvesant appealed to the men in the Dutch towns of Long Island to come to his defense. They didn't come. The reply from Flatbush put it simply: "It is impossible for us to comply . . . as we ourselves are living here on the flatland without any protection and must leave wife and children seated here in fear and trembling, which our hearts would fail to do." On September 8 Stuyvesant surrendered. Claiming New Netherlands for Charles II, Colonel Nicholls named the territory after the king's brother, the Duke of York.

Looking back on it, the period of Dutch control was surprisingly brief: Stuyvesant pulled down the company flag on Manhattan Island only fifty-five years after Henry Hudson had sailed by in search of the Orient, and active colonization lasted actually less than thirty years. But those thirty Dutch years formed the Brooklyn—especially the rural Brooklyn—that was to linger on for nearly two hundred years. The Dutch legacy at its most trivial included such new English words as *stoop*, *cranky*, and *cookie*. At its most significant it stressed the importance of early public education. The Flatbush school the Dutch had founded in the 1650s became Erasmus Hall Academy in the 1780s and, still standing today as Erasmus Hall High School, it can be identified by most Brooklynites as the alma mater of Barbra Streisand. A walk today through the old Reformed Church cemetery across Flatbush Ave-

*Erasmus Hall
High School*

nue from Erasmus reveals stone after weathered eighteenth or nineteenth-century gravestone inscribed in Dutch: *"Hier Lyt Het Lighaam . . . ,"* *"Hier is Begraven . . . ,"* *"Hier rust . . . ."* On an obelisk in a newer corner of the graveyard is one of the earliest English inscriptions: "James H Kerswill born in Flatbush April 12, 1842, Killed June 3, 1864, at the Battle of Cold Harbor, Va., Soldier of the Union." Only then did Dutch Brooklyn fully catch up with the outside world.

But even as Dutch influence waned, the Dutch legacy lingered on as romantic legend and nostalgia. Turn-of-the-century Park Slope millionaires built imitation Dutch mansions along Prospect Park. The Dutch origins of everything from Santa Claus to the baker's dozen were doted on, and Walt Whitman, in his "Brooklyniana" column in the *Standard*, could carry on about "how superior in physical, moral and mental qualities that original stock certainly was" and how, incidentally, the best of them chose to settle in Brooklyn rather than in Manhattan.

A turn-of-the-century mansion, now the Ethical Culture Society Meeting House, on Prospect Park West

The British at first tried pretending the new territory was Yorkshire and divided the colony into three ridings (thridings, thirds), just as they had the Yorkshire back home. Brooklyn and Staten Island were lumped together as West Riding, and Brooklyn didn't become a full-fledged county on its own until 1683, when it became Kings.

The British chose to make their mark on Manhattan, generally ignoring Brooklyn, which they tried—with no noticeable success— to rename Brookland. The Livingstons, a family of Scots who were perhaps more adventurous than their English cousins, built a farm

and a country house on Brooklyn Heights, just across the East
River from the Battery, and a family named Lane ventured as far
as Flatbush. There, they constructed an elaborate Georgian mansion, later named Melrose Hall, which was to become the source
of ghost stories for generations of Flatbush children before it was
torn down in 1903. Brooklyn did provide a few sporting events
for Manhattanites. There was a popular racetrack in Flatlands,
and a bull pit was set up near the ferry, where for a few pennies
bettors could watch a bull take on packs of fighting dogs. In 1752
the colonial legislature met in Brooklyn to avoid the smallpox epi-
demic on the other side of the river. But Brooklyn, when it was
thought of at all, was thought of as the place where the slaughter-
houses were and where the milk and other farm products came
from. Anglo-Saxon Manhattan's attitude toward Dutch Brooklyn
was probably best summed up in the name of the dock on the Manhattan side of the ferry. It was called Dover, after the English
Channel town. To leave from there was to go to a foreign country.

The total population of Kings County in 1776 was about thirty-
seven hundred. Nearly a third of the people were black, and all
but a handful of these were slaves. It was proportionally the highest slave population north of the Mason-Dixon line. Both cotton
and tobacco were grown in Kings County, but slavery—which had
been practiced there since 1640—had followed a different pattern
of development than it did on the Southern plantations. The farms
were smaller, and although two thirds of the white families in
the county owned slaves, most families owned only one. During
the middle of the nineteenth century, when Northerners became
self-conscious about the slaves in their own pasts, Brooklynites
liked to point to this low slave-to-owner ratio to show that the
masters treated their property "just like members of the family."
Indeed, one chronicler of Flatbush's history takes pride in the fact
that blacks were even buried in the Reformed Church burying
ground, although their graves were fenced off in a special section,
of course. Perhaps the slaves themselves did not realize their good
fortune. Reward posters for runaways were common. In 1771,
for instance, Aris Remsen offered a reward of twenty shillings
for a runaway "negro man, Newport, Guinea born, and branded
on the breast with three letters."

A 19th-century notion of how Brooklyn Ferry looked in 1746 (PC)

In August of 1776 Brooklyn underwent the biggest population explosion in its history. In less than a week nearly thirty thousand outsiders—both British and American—swept across the county. The Revolution had begun, and the British, under General William Howe, were about to oust the rebels from New York City. Nearly twelve thousand Americans—mostly from New England and Maryland—were drawn up on Brooklyn Heights and on a line of hills that ran from Newtown Creek through Bedford and Flatbush to the Narrows. The British fleet anchored off Coney Island and Gravesend and on August 25 landed about fifteen thousand men, mostly Hessian mercenaries, but also a few all-black regiments from the West Indies.

One of the American plans for Manhattan involved burning the place down and leaving it, worthless, to the enemy. This was never done, but a modified version of the plan was enacted in Kings County, where the Dutch population had not demonstrated much enthusiasm for George Washington or the Continental Congress. The rebels burned Flatbush farms, and farmers' crops in New Utrecht, Flatlands, and other outlying communities were destroyed so that they would not fall into British hands.

After midnight, on the morning of August 27, the British troops began to move north toward the East River, and an eyewitness later remembered as an old woman that "before noon the Red Coats were so thick in Flatlands you could walk on their heads." But by noon the battle was already over. The American commanders, General Israel Putnam and his subordinate, John Sullivan, were unfamiliar with Brooklyn and had failed to fortify one of the four passes that cut through the hills that separated Gravesend from the East River.

It was a rout. The British poured through the unguarded pass, and there was brief but fierce fighting at the defended passes. Sullivan and General Stirling, whose Marylanders suffered the worst fighting of the battle defending an old stone house near the Gowanus, were captured, along with perhaps a thousand men. A Connecticut militiaman who spent the day watching Brooklyn from a Manhattan rooftop later recalled seeing the Hessians marching toward Brooklyn Ferry. The road was filled with troops for six hours, he remembered, and "to the eye [they] gleamed like sheets of fire." The main body of the American army escaped capture because a storm kept the British fleet out of the East River, and two regiments of Massachusetts fishermen—from Marblehead, Lynn, Salem, and Danvers—managed to row nine thousand men, along with horses, cannon, and ammunition, across the river to Manhattan in a single night. There Washington regrouped his army and fled to safety in White Plains.

The war moved on to the American mainland, but a British army of occupation remained, and after a hundred years of being indifferent to crown rule many Brooklynites suddenly discovered that they were ardent royalists. The Flatlands racetrack was transformed into Ascot Heath. The Livingston family brewery became the King's Brewery, and the Ferry Tavern was renamed King's Head. Red, the badge of loyalty, became *the* fashionable

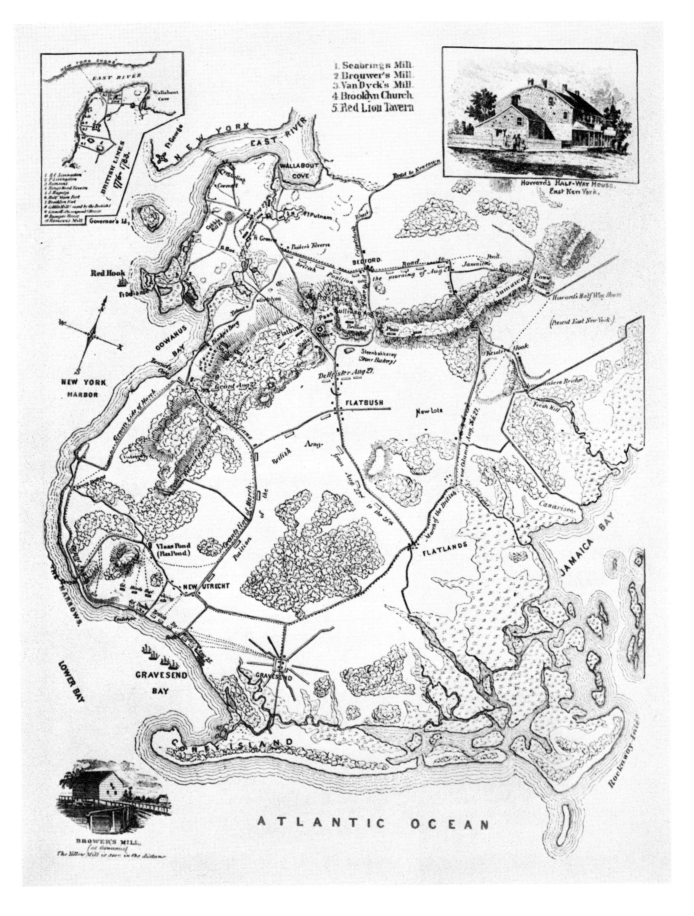

1. Seabrings Mill.
2. Brouwer's Mill.
3. Van Dyck's Mill.
4. Brooklyn Church.
5. Red Lion Tavern.

HOWARD'S HALF-WAY HOUSE,
East New York.

NEW YORK SOUND

EAST RIVER

Wallabout Cove

BRITISH LINES 1776-1783.

Governor's Id.

Ft George

NEW YORK

EAST RIVER

Road to Newtown

WALLABOUT COVE

Ft Putnam

Red Hook

Ft Defiance

BEDFORD

Road to Jamaica

Jamaica

Howard's Half Way House

Pass

GOWANUS BAY

Flatbush

Prospect

Sullivan Aug 27

Pass

Jamaica Pass

(Present East New York)

Keuters Hook

NEW YORK HARBOR

Steenbakkerey
(Stone Bakery)

DeHeister Aug 27

FLATBUSH

New Lots

Fresh Kill

Grant Aug 27

British Army

Marsh

Canarisee

JAMAICA BAY

Vlaas Pond
(Flax Pond)

FLATLANDS

NEW UTRECHT

THE NARROWS

LOWER BAY

GRAVESEND BAY

GRAVESEND

CONEY ISLAND

Rockaway Inlet

ATLANTIC OCEAN

BROWER'S MILL,
(at Gowanus)
The Yellow Mill is seen in the distance.

OPPOSITE, *map of the Battle of Brooklyn, August 27, 1776* (Stiles). *The Vechte-Cortelyou House* LEFT, *built in 1699, was the scene of bitter fighting during the Battle of Brooklyn. Walt Whitman wrote that the "slang name among the boys of Brooklyn" for the stone house was "the old iron nines" because of the wrought iron number on one of the gables. Over the years this somehow changed into "the old iron mines." The present version of the house* ABOVE, *rebuilt by the Parks Department in 1935, stands in a playground on Fifth Avenue which was the home of the Brooklyn Dodgers before the team moved to Ebbets Field in 1913.*

color of the season. Men wore red swatches on their hats, women wore red ribbons, and even slaves, one observer noted, "wore scarlet rags." Red flannel petticoats were said to be in short supply because they had been ripped up to make royalist badges. Even popular sports became politicized. To advertise a bit of Wednesday afternoon bullbaiting at Brooklyn Ferry, a rhymed notice was published:

*Wyckoff-Bennett
House,
built in 1766*

This notice given to all who covet
Baiting the bull and dearly love it,
To-morrow's very afternoon,
At three—or rather not so soon—
A bull of magnitude and spirit
Will dare the dog's presuming merit.
Taurus is steel to the back-bone,

And canine cunning does disown;
The British blood runs through his veins
And barking numbers he disdains.
Sooner than knavish dogs shall rule,
He'll prove himself a true JOHN BULL.

Hundreds of Kings County homes had already been appropriated to house British soldiers. Buildings with two chimneys had first priority because they allowed the family of the house to have the use of one fireplace and the soldiers the exclusive use of the other. The billeted soldiers were, of course, resented, though poorer families appreciated the fact that they provided their own firewood at a time when wood prices were controlled—and some said inflated—by the military government. Before the troops left in 1783, there were a number of marriages between British soldiers and local girls (there was no doubt an eighteenth-century trans-Atlantic version of the World War II English joke that claimed the trouble with the Yanks was that they were overpaid, oversexed, and over here), but the most lasting souvenir of those billeted soldiers is scratched on windowpanes preserved in the old Wycoff-Bennett farmhouse near Gravesend. Two Hessian officers left their names behind: "Toepfer Capt Regt de Ditfurth" and "M Bach Lieutenant v Hessen Hanau Artillerie."

High Tory society centered on Melrose Hall in Flatbush, now the seat of William Axtell, a British colonial, probably from the West Indies, who had married into the wealthy De Peyster family of Manhattan. Axtell gave the most expensive parties in the county, affairs grand enough to lure guests all the way from Manhattan, and was rewarded for his loyalty to the crown with the title of colonel in the Kings County Militia and a phantom regiment—complete with payroll—of five hundred men. In fact Axtell recruited only about thirty men, who set up camp in his front yard and made a general nuisance of themselves. Axtell called them the Nassau Blues. His Flatbush neighbors called them the Nasty Blues, and according to a local clergyman, who was shocked by its blasphemy, the phantom regiment called itself the Holy Ghosters.

Axtell was also responsible for finding quarters for about four hundred Continental Army prisoners of war. Although some of the ghost stories that were to be told about Melrose Hall concerned

American soldiers who supposedly died in chains in the mansion's deep cellars, Axtell actually succeeded in farming out his prisoners to landlords throughout the county, who were paid two dollars a week to feed, house, and keep an eye on their "guests." An English ensign, Thomas Hughes, was offended by the sight of one prisoner he encountered while on a Christmas duck-hunting visit to New Utrecht in 1778. "The ducks are so numerous," he wrote in his journal, "that without exaggeration I am certain I have seen above a thousand of a morn. . . . The people make use of a decoy in winter, by painting their boats white, hiding themselves and then floating like a lump of ice. By this finesse they will get amongst the flocks and kill thirty of a shot." As for the prisoner, "he was very impertinent and answered interrogatories with a contemptuous sneer." What's more, he was dressed "in a blue coat faced red, a brown waistcoat patch'd with all the colours in the rainbow and a greasy pair of leather breaches." The ensign noted with undisguised horror that this "droll diminutive figure," who was employed mending his landlord's trousers, was an *officer*! That shows, he wrote, "what a set of beings some of them are."

The impertinent American lieutenant in his patched waistcoat probably didn't realize how lucky he was. On the other side of Kings County from New Utrecht, in marshy Wallabout Bay on the East River, one of the great atrocities of the war was taking place. There the British had tied up a number of hulks that they used as floating prisons. While it is estimated that about seven thousand men died in battle during the entire war, an additional twelve thousand may have died on the rotting ships with grand old names such as HMS *Whitby* (the first of the hulks), *Prince of Wales*, *Good Hope*, *Stromboli*, *Scorpion*, *Hunter*, and, most notorious of all, *Jersey*.

Thomas Andros was one of the few survivors of HMS *Jersey*. Here is part of his tale:

> When I first became an inmate of this abode of suffering, despair and death, there were about 400 prisoners on board, but in a short time they amounted to 1200. And in proportion to our numbers, the mortality increased. All the most deadly diseases were pressed into the service of the king of horrors, but his prime ministers were dys-

entery, small pox and yellow fever. . . . In a short time we had 200 or more sick and dying lodged in the fore part of the lower gun deck, where all the prisoners were confined at night. Utter derangement was a common symptom of yellow fever, and to increase the horror of the darkness that surrounded us (for we were allowed no lights betwixt decks), the voice of warning would be heard, "Take heed to yourselves. There is a mad man stalking the ship with a knife in his hand." I sometimes found the man a corpse in the morning, by whose side I laid myself down at night. . . . In the morning the hatch-

Middagh Street,
Brooklyn Heights

ways were thrown open and we were allowed to ascend,
all at once, and remain on the upper deck during the day.
But the first object that met our view in the morning was
a most appalling spectacle. A boat loaded with dead
bodies, conveying them to the Long Island shore where
they would be slightly covered with sand.

Although George Washington protested to the British about conditions on the hulks while the war was in progress, the number of
deaths was not appreciated until after the war, when dogs, the
tides, and playing children began to uncover the corpses that had
been quietly buried on the Wallabout shore.

On November 25, 1783, the war in New York ended. The British
fleet sailed out of the harbor. George Washington marched down
Pearl Street in Manhattan to the Battery, where the British had
left their flag flying from a greased pole. The citizens of Kings
County, who in '76 had sworn their gratitude for "His Majesty's
paternal goodness," now begged General Washington "leave to
present you our sincere congratulations on this glorious and ever
memorable era." On Fulton Street, not far from Brooklyn Ferry,
a tavern owner painted the name Benjamin Franklin under a bust
that had previously been honored as George III. The war indeed
was over.

Thirty-one years later Brooklyn again faced up to a British
threat, and this time Kings County left no doubts as to its loyalty.
In August of 1814 word spread that the British fleet was again
going to land at Gravesend Bay and dispatch thousands of troops
who would march across the county as they had in '76 and seize
the harbor. Brooklyn intended to be ready. A craze of fort building
hit the county. On August 10 a committee of tanners and plumbers
began digging earthworks on the hills at Fort Greene and were
soon joined by fire companies, journeyman cabinetmakers, and
twelve hundred Irishmen (who were, a local newspaper reported,
"distinguished by uncommon and well-directed industry"). In a
single day seven hundred and fifty members of the Grand Lodge
of Free and Accepted Masons—headed by no less a figure than
De Witt Clinton himself—built Fort Masonic, the password of the
day being "The Grand Master expects every Mason to do his duty."
From Bushwick, New Utrecht, Flatlands, and other villages com-

mittees of diggers were organized. In what must have been one of the earliest all-female demonstrations in the history of the Republic "200 ladies" formed a procession and marched to the earthworks to labor with the men. Entire congregations, led by their pastors, dug away on the chain of hills that the British had crossed with such little difficulty during the Revolution. From across the river Tammany Hall turned out 1,150 volunteers. Others came from Connecticut and New Jersey.

Samuel Woodworth, the renowned lyricist of "The Old Oaken Bucket," was inspired to write a new song, "The Patriotic Diggers," copies of which could be purchased for six cents at the *Long Island Star* newspaper office. Addressed to "Johnny Bull" and intended to be sung to the tune of "Great Way Off at Sea," it warned:

> To protect our rights
> 'Gainst your flints and triggers,
> See on Brooklyn Heights
> Our patriotic diggers;
> Men of every age,
> Color, rank, profession,
> Ardently engage
> Labor in succession.
> Pickaxe, shovel, spade,
> Crowbar, hoe, and barrow,
> Better not invade,
> Yankees have the marrow.

And they didn't invade. After a month of furious digging the craze ended and the diggers went home. The British never did appear, and eventually the War of 1812 itself wound down. One of the choruses of Woodworth's anthem boasted "Better not invade;/Recollect the Spirit/which our dads displayed,/And their sons inherit." But the sons, in fact, displayed more spirit than their dads, however faddish it was, because they had a sense of community and nation that their fathers had never known.

In the years between the two wars with Britain the Brooklyn boom had begun. From the end of the Revolutionary War to 1835 the population of Kings County jumped from five thousand to thirty-two thousand, with most of the newcomers settling in the

East River towns of Brooklyn and its next door neighbor Williamsburgh. By 1855, with over two hundred thousand inhabitants, the new City of Brooklyn—which now included Williamsburgh and Bushwick—would be the third largest in the nation. Many of the new Brooklynites came from Germany and Ireland, and before long there was a so-called German Town near Wallabout Bay and an Irish Town below the Heights, near the ferry dock. But the greatest wave of immigrants came not from across the sea but from New England, and suspicious contributors to the letters-to-the-editor columns warned of Yankee "invasions" from Connecticut, Massachusetts, and Vermont.

As it grew, Brooklyn found that urbanization was far from painless. An 1818 guidebook to New York failed to see its appeal. "Extricate yourself from the narrow, dirty and disagreeable streets of Brooklyn with all possible dispatch," it advised and suggested climbing the nearest hill to enjoy the view of Manhattan and the harbor. The *Long Island Star*, which was published in Brooklyn, agreed. "No spot in the world," it editorialized, "calls more

A Methodist missionary from Manhattan tries to save souls on Wallabout Bay in 1787 (Sands)

loudly for improvement." Improvement began with the town's first municipal laws, passed in 1821, and they were basic enough: Landlords had to provide sidewalks (of brick, stone, or gravel); bread was required to be accurately weighed and made from "wholesome flour," or the baker risked a 10¢ per loaf fine; a fire watch was established; and sheep, hogs, and bulls were not permitted to run at large (risking fines of 25¢, $3, and $4, respectively).

Housing was scarce, and since, as James Fenimore Cooper commented, "No American, who is at all comfortable in life, will share his dwelling with another," there began a rush to build low-cost one-family houses that would continue into the mid-1850s. With so much construction the town's streets, complained the *News*, were "cluttered with bricks and mortar and lumber." The demand for real estate was so great that downtown churches were selling off their cemetery land for a thousand dollars an acre, while Hezekiah Beers Pierpont, who owned sixty acres on Brooklyn Heights, offered twenty-five-by-a-hundred-foot lots ("A select neighborhood and circle of society") which, he advertised, were ideally located for businessmen who had to make the daily commute to Manhattan on the new steam ferry. In less select neighborhoods beyond the Heights, where the air presumably was not nearly so fresh, cheap wooden houses were being thrown up at the rate of two hundred a year.

The typical Brooklyn house was changing from the familiar Dutch farmhouse to a wooden cottage standing on a large lot to unbroken blocks of stone and brick row houses. Many of the houses in outlying districts (especially in Williamsburgh, which had begun as a real estate development named after the developer's friend, Colonel Jonathan Williams, Benjamin Franklin's grandnephew) were constructed en masse by speculative builders whose sales technique often involved offering a congregation a site for a church without cost. The site was usually at the center of the builder's tract, and in keeping with the theory that population followed churches, once the church was established, the lots around it sold off quickly. Through such schemes Brooklyn was well on its way to becoming the City of Churches, as the town fathers liked to call it later in the century. Other builders, such as Walter Whitman, Sr., and his sons, George, Andrew, and Walt (though the

*Fulton Street
near Brooklyn
Ferry, ca. 1857*
(PC)

poet later claimed to have been a laboring carpenter, he was actually an out-of-work newspaperman acting as the family book-
keeper), simply built a house at a time, which they would live in
until it became profitable to sell, after which they would move on
to the next. On one house they might clear six hundred dollars and
on another as much as thirty-five hundred.

But what drew people to Brooklyn was not only inexpensive
housing and an easy commute to Manhattan. Brooklyn had discovered its waterfront. In 1801 the government had opened the
Navy Yard in Wallabout Bay, where the prison hulks had once
floated, and after the War of 1812 a number of privately owned
shipbuilding docks started to appear along the river. Rope-making
factories were soon opened to outfit the ships. There were new glue
factories and a glassworks. Hezekiah Pierpont built a wind-driven
gin distillery, others quickly followed, and by 1855 distilling alco-

hol was the most profitable business in the city. Sugar refineries opened, as did leather-goods factories and hat-making operations. There were whale-oil refineries and several breweries, so jammed along the river that from Manhattan, Brooklyn looked to one early journalist like a walled city. (A writer for *Harper's Magazine,* obviously a more romantic sort, thought the jumble of docks and factories resembled "Rhineish castles.")

In 1854, however, Brooklyn's economy slowed, and the bottom dropped out of the building boom, with houses being sold off for as much as 30 percent below cost. The river communities—from Greenpoint with its refineries through Williamsburgh with its breweries and sugar mills to Brooklyn with its docks—were soon crowded with men working or looking for work. With the coming of the Civil War the city would see its first labor unrest. Two of the new grain elevators at Atlantic Basin were burned by a systematic band of about two hundred men ("There was not a sign of disorderly conduct," the *New York Tribune* noted. "Everything transpired peaceably") who were believed to be former grain shovelers put out of work by machines that could move, screen, and bag two thousand bushels an hour.

Abraham Lincoln did not carry Kings County in the election of 1860. Abolition and the new Republican Party were not popular in either Brooklyn or New York City, and it took an upstate landslide to win the election that year for Lincoln. Brooklyn was considered proslavery. The *Brooklyn Daily Eagle*'s loyalty was so much in doubt that when war broke out the newspaper lost its right to use the mails until it changed editors. The *Brooklyn City News* claimed a vote for Lincoln would put in doubt "whether white men shall govern the country," while a Brooklyn assemblyman, a Democrat, argued the legalistic point that since "colored persons are not citizens of the United States . . . they have no right to claim full priviledges of citizenship in this state." Even the city's most famous preacher, the Reverend Henry Ward Beecher, asked, "Are we ready to receive four millions of blacks . . . to compete with the present occupants of the labor market now over stocked?" To keep matters ecumenical, the Roman Catholic archbishop John Hughes warned that if Catholics were asked "to fight for the abolition of slavery . . . they [would] turn away in disgust."

For most Brooklyn voters slavery was indeed an economic ques-

ABOVE, *an 1859 view of the Brooklyn water works from Ridgewood Reservoir in Queens, showing Cypress Hills Cemetery, the Union Race Course, and the village of East New York. East New York, Walt Whitman observed, afforded "superior inducements to families who desire to be just out of the city, and yet within an hour's reach of it." (NYHS)* BELOW, *a Chinese corner of the Cypress Hills Cemetery today.*

tion, and not an ethical one. In the census of 1860, 40 percent of Brooklyn's 267,000 citizens were foreign-born, 57,000 of them Irish and 24,000 German. They had reason to fear the freed black competition Beecher warned of. As for their bosses, the South owed the banks, merchants, and mill owners of New York and Brooklyn nearly $200,000,000, which would be forfeited if there was war. The South was also the major market for goods shipped from New York Harbor, and Southerners were the chief buyers of Brooklyn-made carriages and harnesses. On both sides of the East River factories produced cheap cotton cloth "exclusively for the southern trade." Even Confederate Army uniforms and Confederate money were manufactured in cities on New York Harbor.

When the mayor of New York called for the establishment of a free city that would stay out of war and trade evenly with both sides, he was cheered by newspaper editorials in Charleston, Richmond, and Brooklyn, but not in New York City. Another suggestion was that all of Long Island secede to become an independent state with Brooklyn as its capital (a plan attacked by Walt Whitman because it would mean an increase in Brooklyn city taxes). In 1861 Jefferson Davis received a letter (somehow leaked to the press) which threatened that if war broke out, two hundred "influential citizens" of New York and Brooklyn would seize the Navy Yard and key forts and declare the harbor neutral territory.

In April 1861 war did break out, but the Navy Yard did not fall. Instead fifty thousand men turned out at Fort Greene Park to answer Lincoln's call for volunteers. There was no more talk of secession or neutrality. Before the end of the month three regiments had left Brooklyn for the war, the most famous being the 14th Regiment (84th NY Volunteers), which fought in both battles of Bull Run and at Gettysburg, the Wilderness, and Spotsylvania. Its commander had the good political fortune to be captured by the rebels at Bull Run I and then released in time to get back to Brooklyn and be elected mayor in 1863. One Brooklyn unit, mostly German, was called the Schwartze Jaeger, and there were also the Irish Legion and a company of Zouaves made up mostly of city firemen. The first Brooklyn casualty, or at least the first celebrated casualty, was Clarence Mackenzie, a twelve-year-old drummer boy, who was properly, and gloomily, buried with his drum in Green-Wood Cemetery. The fact that he was killed not by

Rebs but accidentally by fellow Yanks didn't dim the occasion's grand Victorian pomp. In battle the Confederates did find their mark, however. Of the 1,000 members of the Brooklyn Phalanx that marched down to the ferry in 1861, only 234 returned three years later.

In 1864 the society ladies of Brooklyn found a patriotic project to engage their zeal. The women of Cincinnati had raised $240,000 for the Sanitary Commission, a forerunner of the Red Cross, and challenged Brooklyn to beat their record. On Washington's Birthday in 1864 the Great Sanitary Fair opened at the Brooklyn Academy of Music on Montague Street, and two temporary buildings were put up nearby. Modeled on London's Crystal Palace exhibition, the fair featured displays of modern machinery, cattle shows, exhibits of curiosities and relics from the Orient (to "excite the envy of a Barnum"), art shows, military band concerts, an official exhibition newspaper (*Drum-Taps*), and a mammoth painting— illuminated by a thousand gas jets—of a sanitary commission battlefield hospital at work. The most popular exhibit of the fair was the New England Kitchen, a reproduction of an eighteenth- century Yankee farmhouse where costumed waitresses served clam chowder, corn bread, and baked beans. When it closed in March with a Calico Ball, the fair had raised over $400,000, and the now patriotic *Eagle* called it "the greatest event of the year." Not only had Brooklyn nearly doubled Cincinnati's contribution, it had also organized its fair before New York got around to staging one of its own. To one observer this was "the first great act of self- assertion ever made by the City of Brooklyn."

The greatest—or at least the most unsettling—event of 1863 for New York City was the Draft Riots, when unrest over draft laws that allowed the rich to buy their way out of military service boiled over and white rioters vented their frustration by attacking blacks and even burning down an orphanage for black children. When word of the Manhattan outrages reached Flatbush, local blacks, some of whom were still only Dutch-speaking, fearfully barricaded themselves in a four-story windmill, the tallest struc- ture on Long Island. While no mob came for them, black workers at the Lorillard and Watson tobacco factories near Brooklyn Ferry were not as fortunate. Lorillard employed both blacks and whites, Watson only blacks. In August, just a month after the Manhattan riots, white demonstrators appeared at Lorillard's gates and demanded that the blacks be fired. (The *New York Herald* later said the trouble was caused by abolitionists who were encouraging the blacks to become "insolent and insulting." The *New York World*, on the other hand, blamed antiabolitionist newspapers for encouraging hatred against the black workers in the Irish neighborhood where the factories were located.) Lorillard officials knuckled under, and the mob, which numbered between two and three thousand, moved on to the Watson plant, where they smashed windows and broke in the doors. The black workers retreated to the second floor, and while the mob was trying to set the building on fire police arrived and, according to the *World*, "proceeded to quell the riot by clubbing the negroes."

A year earlier a Brooklyn horsecar conductor had refused to take a black's money and ordered him to get off. He stayed put and, after he was thrown off, sued. In a court decision that sounds like a civil rights case from the late 1950s, the judge ruled that the black had every right to ride the car and awarded him damages: 6¼¢.

Brooklyn seemed to be maintaining its reputation for being antiblack. Under New York State's emancipation law slaves could have been freed as early as 1788, but Brooklyn's first freedman, Caesar Foster, did not win his freedom until 1797. The last slave set free in Kings County is believed to have been Sam Anderson of Flatbush, who was released in 1822. But Brooklyn's harsh reputation may have been unfair. One of the original landowners of Bushwick in 1660 was "Francisco the Negro," although little seems known of him but his name. One of the first dominies of Breukelen raised Dutch eyebrows by including black children in his Sunday school, and the New African Society for Mutual Relief, one of the country's first all-black abolitionist societies, was founded in Brooklyn in 1808. Nearly fifty years later Brooklyn's Henry Ward Beecher became one of the most famous abolitionists in the nation when, to outrage his congregation, he auctioned off a slave named Sarah from the pulpit of Plymouth Church in Brooklyn Heights. He provoked a different kind of outrage when he raised money to buy guns—which became known as Beecher's Bibles—for John Brown.

There is the usual list of black firsts in Brooklyn: the first black

home owner (James Ash of 41 Hicks Street, 1804), the first black doctor (Gilbert Gilberts, 1810), the first black school (1815), the first black church (1816). But the most important black first was the establishment early in the nineteenth century of Weeksville, an independent community of free middle-class blacks on Crow Hill, on the edge of what is today one of the largest black neighborhoods in the country, Bedford-Stuyvesant.

With the war winding down and a Northern victory clearly in sight, someone in Washington decided to stage a patriotic flag raising at Fort Sumter in Charleston Harbor. Major-General Robert Anderson, whose surrender of the fort had marked the beginning of the war, would raise the same American flag he had lowered four years earlier, and Henry Ward Beecher, whose Sunday sermons had become Brooklyn's major tourist attraction,

A photograph from the 1920s of the last remaining houses of the Weeksville settlement, probably built in the 1830s
(LIHS)

would be the chief orator, supposedly requested by President Lincoln himself.

In Brooklyn a committee was immediately organized to charter a boat so that the city would be represented at the ceremony. The only available boat was the small—and, as it turned out, unsteady—*Oceanus*, a "propeller" (as opposed to a side-wheeler) steamboat that usually made the New York to Providence, Rhode Island, run. The one hundred and eighty Brooklynites chosen to make the voyage were, according to a contemporary historian, a "very select and *recherché*" company who spent their three days at sea singing "We are out on the ocean sailing," "John Brown's soul is marching on," and "We'll hang Jeff Davis to a sour apple tree" when they weren't being seasick. Actually they spent much of their time being seasick. Just before they left New York Harbor, word arrived that Lee had surrendered to Grant, and later the party aboard the *Oceanus* claimed to have been the first to bring the news to Charleston.

With peace and the mustering out of thousands of young soldiers who had left their farms and small towns for the first time, cities on New York Harbor were more attractive to newcomers than ever. Beecher, in a sermon published just after the war ended, warned them away.

> I dread nothing more than to hear young men saying, "I am going to the city. . . ." If a man's bones are made of flint, if his muscles are made of leather; if he can work sixteen or eighteen hours a day and not wink, and then sleep scarcely winking—if in other words, he is built for mere toughness, then he can go into the city and go through the ordeal which business and professional men are obliged to go through who succeed. . . . There are ten men that can succeed in the country where there is one that can succeed in the city.

But Beecher was preaching to a congregation of comfortable Brooklyn Heights businessmen whose egos were no doubt boosted by the thought that they were that rare breed of city men who had succeeded.

A different picture of the variety and richness of postwar Brook-

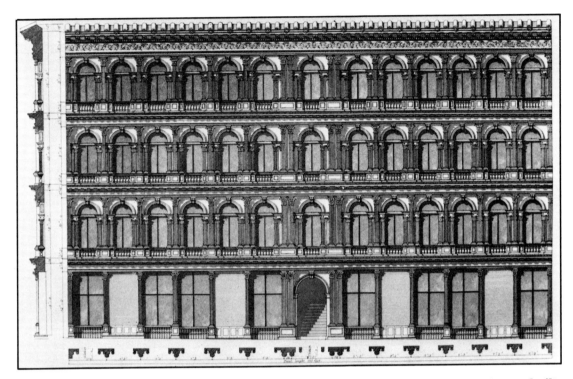

The Halsey Building (later called Dieter's Hotel and the Arbuckle Building) was built on Fulton Street facing City Hall Park in 1857. The prefabricated cast-iron facade came from Daniel Badger's Architectural Iron Works in Manhattan, and this illustration appeared in the company's 1865 catalog of "Iron Architecture." Badger himself lived in Brooklyn, and one of his former employees—Niels Poulson, founder of the Hecla Iron Works in Greenpoint—constructed an all-metal mansion in Bay Ridge. The Halsey Building was destroyed in 1955 to make way for the New York State Supreme Court Building. (PC)

lyn city life can be guessed from a list of "local characters" compiled by an amateur historian who lived in Williamsburgh:

> Bismarck used to run through the streets of the 16th Ward, giving commands to an imaginary army. The butchers and pretzel bakers were in the habit of decorating him with frankfurters and pretzels.

> "Matches," the little hunchback Hebrew, who peddled the old time sulphur matches, three boxes for five cents. If a customer kept on dickering with him long enough, he could get seven packs for five cents. "Matches" was not more than three feet tall.

> John Tassel, the human ostrich.

Louise Herman, the vamp, who wandered around Stagg Street and vicinity day and night.

John Camble, a colored man, drove a cart. He always whistled and was called Happy Jack. During the Civil War, in '63 or '64, he escaped from a mob, eager to hang him, by swimming from New York to Williamsburgh.

Billy Wheeler sold oysters, he carried two pails on chains from his shoulders.

The fish peddlers, with hand scales, were followed by all the cats of the neighborhood.

Local characters in the vicinity of Grand Street were Apple Mary, the Yellow Kid, Crazy George and Clarence the Cop.

Swamp Barbel always expected her fortune to arrive. Store keepers gave her boxes filled with all kinds of trash, telling her that they contained the money which she expected to get.

Uncle Sam was George Veritzan, a plumber, located on Broadway. He travelled to Albany, Washington, and other cities as Uncle Sam. His services as Uncle Sam were constantly required all over the country.

Nigger Tom sold hot corn every night on the streets from a hot boiler.

Old Pat, the tinker who mended leaky pots and kettles.

Ed and John, the colored chimney sweeps.

The sandman who sold white floor sand.

Lins the soap dealer at Bartlett Street sold a shiny soft soap at ten cents a bucketful.

"Mr. White," the straw-man, used to drive his wagon through the streets selling straw. He always had "white pants" covering his horses legs.

During these postwar years Brooklyn was going through that most modern of problems, an oil crisis. Early in the century there

had been great concern about what would happen when there was no more whale oil to burn, but the problem was solved in 1854 by the introduction of Kerosene, with a capital *K*. *Kerosene* is a Brooklyn word, a brand name coined by Abraham Gesner, a Williamsburgh refiner, for his highly combustible lamp oil. Kerosene may have solved the problem of the diminishing supply of whale oil, but it created a new problem: It was *so* highly combustible—and had such a low flash point—that the heat from a lamp's flame could ignite the lamp's Kerosene reservoir and create a dangerous little bomb. The new lamp oil was burning down more houses than Abraham Gesner cared to admit.

In the 1870s Charles Pratt introduced a new oil that had a flash point of between 125 and 150 degrees Fahrenheit, making it, as the Pratt advertisements said, the oil that would not explode—at least in everyday use. Pratt had refineries in Williamsburgh and Greenpoint, where his docks received barge loads of crude oil and shipped out barrels of refined "Safe and Best" Astral Oil (which most people still called kerosene). After 1879 a Rockefeller-owned pipeline stretched directly from the Pennsylvania oil fields to the

Charles Pratt's Astral Oil Works, ca. 1875 (LIHS)

Brooklyn plant. By then Pratt had bought up or driven out of business most of the competing refineries in Brooklyn—there had been more than fifty in 1875—and had already sold his company, secretly, to John D. Rockefeller.

Pratt was one of those self-made city businessmen whom Beecher preached about. He kept shipping costs down by breaking the coopers' union and controlling the price of barrels. He ran imaginative advertisements in which travelers to such faraway places as Tibet or Jerusalem reported that their lamps had been lit by Pratt's oil. He founded the Pratt Institute to "help all classes of workers, artists, apprentices, and homemakers" (in the 1930s the institute would become a college specializing in the arts, engineering, and design) and in 1886 built the Astral Apartments in Greenpoint. The six-story apartment building, whose exotic-sounding location was—and still remains—between Java and India streets, was one of the city's first tenements. Designed for the "deserving poor," the Astral came equipped with a library (where the inscription over the fireplace read "Waste neither time nor money"), a kindergarten, and a model cottage with a housekeeper "to demonstrate to the residents a wholesome and simple home life," as one old Greenpointer phrased it.

Pratt's inspiration for the Astral Apartments was Alfred Tredway White's Tower and Home Apartments, which had, in turn, been inspired by some experiments in workers' housing White had seen in London. The apartments, built in what was then Red Hook but is now called Cobble Hill, might be considered the first low-

Entrance to the Astral Apartments

RIGHT, *Alfred Tredway White's Riverside Building, in Brooklyn Heights,* and LEFT, *Workingmen's Cottages, in Cobble Hill*

rent housing project in New York. With its decorative brick and its open ironwork stairs and balconies it is certainly the most durably attractive. When it opened in 1879, the 226 two-to-five room apartments rented for from $1.80 to $3.50 a week (plus 30¢ for each time you took a bath in the cellar bathrooms). Down the street from the Tower Apartments, White built a court of 34 six-room Workingman's Cottages (each 11½ feet wide), which rented for $18 a month. White was a philanthropist whose motto was "Philanthropy plus 5 percent," and indeed, the Apartments, the Cottages, and the Riverside Buildings, which he later built on the edge of Brooklyn Heights, all made their profit.

Behind the industrial wall that ran along the East River rural

Brooklyn lived on. The cities of New York and Brooklyn were still fed largely by Kings County and Long Island farms. The iron water pump next to the Grand Street ferry in Williamsburgh was called the Black Cow because so many farmers paused there to water their milk before shipping it on to Manhattan. Flatbush was no longer as isolated as it had been when the two big events of its day were the stagecoach leaving for Brooklyn at eight in the morning and returning at four in the afternoon. The coaches had been replaced by horse-drawn omnibuses (every hour on the hour for downtown Brooklyn) and later by the horse-drawn streetcars of the Brooklyn City Railway Company, which by 1882 employed 1,500 men and 2,500 horses to keep its 625 cars running. But Flatbush was still a country town, and its newspaper was aptly named *The Rural Gazette*.

Even with improved transportation, Flatbush and the other outlying towns were far removed from the bustle of the waterfront. To get to the Manhattan ferries, people from Gravesend, Flatlands, and New Utrecht had to get first to Flatbush or, later, to take a steam train to the Brooklyn city line, near Fort Hamilton on the Narrows, where they could transfer to a streetcar. Progress meant that Cypress Hills Plank Road was paved and renamed Cypress Hills Macadamized Road and then paved again to become Cypress Hills Avenue. Yet for the people of Greenpoint, the shops on Fulton Street in downtown Brooklyn were still an hour's streetcar ride away. Even as late as the 1890s *Harper's Magazine* reported, there were people in the remote German-speaking sections of Williamsburgh who had never seen the Brooklyn Bridge and who had to hire "petty neighborhood lawyers" when forced to deal with the outside world.

One of the outsiders those lawyers may have had to deal with was Hugh McLaughlin, who for more than thirty years was the boss of Brooklyn's Democratic machine. ("Political machinery," the *Eagle* once noted in explaining how Hughey operated, "is simply organization.") McLaughlin had begun his political career as one of the party organizers who got out the vote for Stephen A. Douglas in the 1860 election. Like many good party men, he had a secure but hardly demanding job at the Navy Yard, the yard being, according to the *Eagle*, the traditional "snug harbor for faithful political workers." Over the next decade McLaughlin rose to the top in Kings County politics, left the Navy Yard, and set up his

unofficial court first in the county coroner's office and then at Kerrigan's Auction Rooms on Willoughby Street. Although he was never to hold public office, he became the man who ruled Brooklyn.

Paerdegaat Creek, Flatlands, at the turn of the century (LIHS)

To get anything done in the city, the standard advice was, "Go and see Hughey." Party hacks appeared regularly at Kerrigan's and, less regularly, so did the likes of Henry Ward Beecher. A reporter who watched McLaughlin at work wrote that he was "a man of few words. When he does speak he is apt to talk in parables. Office seekers say he is a good listener." His comments, in fact, tended to amount to little more than "All right" or "Go ahead" or "I wouldn't." But they could also be more oracular, such as "People want a young man for mayor" or "People want a soldier for sheriff." And it would be arranged. On a more practical level he was the man who picked the aldermen. Although "mayor of Brooklyn" was a grand title, it was an empty one. Aldermen—most of whom were familiar faces at Kerrigan's—had the power, and Hughey had the aldermen.

The new city charter of 1882—one that would be copied by cities throughout the country—made life a little more difficult for the boys at Kerrigan's. The charter established the mayor as the true head of city government, with the power to hire and fire everyone from police commissioner to tax collector. As a result municipal elections were popular as they never had been before, and more people turned out to vote for mayor than for governor (although some of those voters were said to be Manhattanites brought over for the day by McLaughlin and his friends). The first mayor under this new system, which stripped aldermen of most of their power, was that unheard-of thing in Brooklyn politics, a Republi-

The corner of Fourth Avenue and 98th Street (now called Marine Avenue) in Bay Ridge, 1898 (LIHS)

can. He was a thirty-two-year-old millionaire named Seth Low, who would spend his life being everyone's favorite reformer, first in Brooklyn, then as president of Columbia University, and finally as mayor of New York (beginning in 1901, after the consolidation of the five boroughs). The Lows were a Brooklyn family that had made its fortune in the clipper-ship trade bringing silk from China, and young Seth was viewed by his admirers with almost messianic fervor. ("A man of sterling Christian principle," one wrote, "and of the purest and noblest character.") Even his birth was given tragically pious overtones: "With her hands devoutly laid upon his head," we are told, his mother "in almost her last breath commended him to the blessing of God, and died serenely...."

While the crowd at Kerrigan's was biding its time and Low was reforming the public school system, throwing scoundrels out of office, and trying to wipe out the city's considerable debt, the great bridge that towered over the ferry dock at the foot of Fulton Street was nearing completion. Its official name was the New York and Brooklyn Bridge, although its builder called it the East River Bridge, and Currier & Ives, on one of their prints, the *Great* East River Bridge. But to the people of Brooklyn it was and would remain simply "the bridge." Later bridges would have names, but even today when a Brooklyn cab driver asks, "Want me to take the bridge?" he is not referring to the Manhattan Bridge or the Williamsburg or the Verrazano-Narrows (which is always called the Verrazano and never the Narrows). He is talking about the Brooklyn Bridge.

Brooklyn had a Bridge Street long before there was any plan for a bridge across the East River. It turned off Fulton Street and ran as pure propaganda toward the river: If there was a Bridge Street, surely, sooner or later, there would have to be a bridge. Talk of one sort of East River bridge or another had been common since the turn of the century, and after the Civil War a man named Julius Adams, an expert on sewer construction, received a good deal of attention with a scheme in which two elliptical tubes, rather like sewer pipes, would be supported by "ribbons of steel" as they arched their way between Brooklyn and Manhattan. The *Eagle* beat its editorial drums for a bridge, but it was the savage winter of 1866 that seemed finally to make a bridge a certainty. The ice on the river was so treacherous that year that ferryboats often remained at their docks, and the cliché of the season was that it was easier to get to Albany than to Manhattan.

In April 1867 the New York Bridge Company, a private corporation with the power to issue stock, began searching for a bridge to build. In his proposal to the company John Roebling—a German immigrant who had perfected an ingenious method of weaving wire like rope to produce the strongest cables ever manufactured—wrote:

> The contemplated work, when constructed in accordance with my design, will not only be the greatest bridge in existence, but it will be the greatest engineering work of this continent, and of the age. Its most conspicuous features, the towers, will serve as landmarks to the adjoining cities, and they will be entitled to be ranked as national monuments.

And this was correct, every word of it. Although one of Roebling's early sketches for the towers had them looking like entrances to Egyptian tombs, and a later design had rounded Romanesque arches, at the last minute he pushed the arches up and made them Gothic. America had its greatest cathedral.

To finance the bridge Brooklyn bought $3,000,000 worth of Bridge Company stock, and New York, which considered its interest in the project to be just about half of Brooklyn's, invested $1,500,000. Another $500,000 was invested by private individuals. Construction dragged on for fourteen years while the costs mounted. As the extent of the involvement of Boss Tweed—the larcenous mayor of New York—and other grafters became known some curious stock dealings were discovered to have taken place, including the circulation of counterfeit certificates—which was probably the origin of the notion that a sucker is someone who would buy the Brooklyn Bridge. For a time you *could* buy the bridge, or at least a piece of it, in the form of stock, even if you might lose your shirt doing so.

At least twenty men were killed building the bridge, although the company never kept an exact count. One of them was John Roebling, who died, in what seems like an excess of ironic symbolism, after a ferryboat crushed his foot. He may have been the first casualty of the war between bridges and boats, but he was on

Currier & Ives' lithograph of "The Great East River Bridge to Connect the Cities of New York & Brooklyn" was published in 1872, when only the foundations of the two stone towers were completed. The lithographer gave the yet-to-be-built towers rounded romanesque arches rather than the pointed gothic ones that would appear on the finished bridge. (PC)

the winning side. There were thirteen ferry lines crossing the river when the bridge opened in 1883; sixty years later the last one went out of business.

After John Roebling's death in 1869, his son, Washington, who had graduated from Rensselaer Polytechnic Institute and learned the science of tunnel digging as an engineer in the Civil War, took over and directed the work until he came down with a case of the "bends" while supervising the digging of the caisson (underwater foundation) of the Brooklyn tower. After that he stayed in his apartment on Columbia Heights (in the same building where Hart Crane would later write *The Bridge*) and watched the progress of the construction through a spyglass. His wife, Emily, taught herself engineering and visited the bridge every day to become his eyes on the job. In a very real sense Emily was the Roebling who finished the bridge.

The stone towers of the completed bridge stood 1,595 feet and 6 inches apart, making the structure the longest suspension bridge in the world. The foundation of the tower on the Brooklyn side stood on solid rock, while that on the Manhattan side—try as the engineers had to find rock—rested on hard-packed gravel. At the bridge's center the roadway was 135 feet above high tide, a figure which, because the Navy Yard was upriver from the span, was to influence the height of masts on American Navy ships for generations.

Opening Day was May 24, 1883, Queen Victoria's birthday, a coincidence that led to an Irish boycott of the festivities. President Chester A. Arthur, however, was on hand and heard the principal speaker of the day, a future mayor of New York, extol as a sign of progress the fact that a typical worker on the bridge made $2.50 a day. The builders of the pyramids, he claimed, worked at a per diem rate of 2¢. The ceremonies ended with a Heights clergyman thanking the Almighty that Brooklyn was finally united "with all that is delightful" in Manhattan. A week after the opening a

Memorial Day crowd panicked when someone shouted that the bridge was falling. Twelve people were trampled to death, and thirty-five others were injured. A year later P. T. Barnum, never one to pass up an opportunity, drove a herd of twenty-one elephants, including his star attraction, Jumbo, across to test the safety of the bridge. It passed.

With the bridge open another step in an unwritten master plan for Brooklyn was complete. For men like James S. T. Stranahan—a leading bridge advocate and a city commissioner who lived to see a statue of himself grace the entrance to Prospect Park—Brooklyn had a destiny. While the nation talked about its manifest destiny to stretch its boundaries westward to the Pacific Ocean, Stranahan believed Brooklyn's destiny was to stretch eastward to the Atlantic Ocean, to absorb Flatbush, Coney Island, and the other oceanfront towns and to fill the boundaries of Kings County.

OPPOSITE, *a* Puck *cartoonist in 1883 predicted the opening ceremonies of the bridge on May 24 would include a crush of newspaper editors and publishers, eager politicians (including President Arthur), party hacks, Masons, and local gadabouts. Boycotting the festivities is a tugboat full of Irishmen.* (PC) LEFT, *another, perhaps more sublime view of the grand opening.* (PC)

The Bridge today

The ambitious road-building projects that accompanied the creation of Prospect Park in the early 1870s would help to strengthen the river communities' ties with the ocean towns. The bridge was to extend those ties across the river to Manhattan.

Back in the 1820s James Fenimore Cooper had dismissed Brooklyn as "a suburb differently governed," and in the 1890s Julian Ralph would write that any fad that swept Manhattan was sure to sweep Brooklyn so long as it wasn't expensive and didn't involve going to the theater. Those condescending judgments would not have bothered Stranahan. Brooklyn, to him, was not intended to be in competition with Manhattan. Its destiny was to be a suburb, but a suburb that would be part of the city itself, a suburb so large in land and population that it would in fact dominate the entire city.

Julian Ralph was probably best known for his magazine articles about the American West, many of which had been illustrated by his friend Frederic Remington, but in 1893 *Harper's Magazine* sent him over to Brooklyn to have a look around. "Every other city," he wrote, "earns its own way, while Brooklyn works for New York and is paid off like a shop-girl on Saturday night." It was a city dominated by women, where bowling (seventy bowling clubs listed in the *Eagle*), choral singing, churchgoing (rather than theatergoing), and politics were the chief local amusements. Brooklyn men, he noted, even let women enter their private clubs. (Which was true to a limited extent. At the Montauk Club a special entrance—not quite so grand as the front door—and a private parlor were set aside for members' wives, while at another Park Slope club, the Riding and Driving, women were allowed full privileges, including participation in the annual Roman Circus in the club's indoor riding ring.)

Manhattan, Ralph wrote, was for the very rich and the very poor and above all for the unmarried. "Many a countryman who comes to New York and prospers never masters the metropolis or feels safe in it. Sooner or later such ones move to Brooklyn."

He continued, "It's a woman's town. By day there are no men in those endless miles of dwellings. The women have the city to them-

Laying the cornerstone of the Montauk Club in 1890, a detail from the frieze over the front door of the Park Slope clubhouse

selves and rule over children, maids, nurses, shade trees, flowers and pretty dooryards." In the Fulton Street shopping district, he wrote, "carriages are few . . . and policemen gain the appearance of giants among so many women. Indeed the crowds of ladies pouring in and out the great doorways set the fanciful spectator to imagining what Eden might have been were Adam and his part in life dispensed with."

Although he mentioned the two thousand ships that docked each year in Brooklyn, Ralph missed a significant side to the city in his reveries of a suburban Eden without Adam. Brooklyn had a very unladylike tradition of waterfront brawling. Back in 1827 the *Long Island Star* had observed: "Nothing flourishes there but meeting-houses and porter houses; the women fill the former and the men the latter." For over a century Sands Street, the avenue that ran to the gates of the Navy Yard, would be famous with sailors throughout the world for its bars, girls, and tattoo parlors.

A privately funded sociological survey of the Red Hook and the South Brooklyn waterfront written a few years after Ralph's article noted that the chief problems of the neighborhood were truant children, the "immodesty of the young girls," and drunkenness ("especially drunken sailors"). Even worse than the saloons as "breeding places of thievery, hold-ups and the forming of vicious habits," the report noted, were Red Hook's twenty-two poolrooms. There were also three dance halls frequented by sailors and "women over thirty," many of whom were believed to be "dope fiends," the evidence being that the customers "were dull and heavy, danced very little and listened to wretched music." The report recommended the establishment of "English-style coffee houses" to help remedy all this.

The "endless miles of dwellings" that Ralph mentioned were indeed spreading out from downtown Brooklyn, and the farther they got from the waterfront the more ornate they became. The classically austere Federal and Greek-Revival façades of pre-Civil War Brooklyn Heights were no match for the brick and sandstone busywork of the new row houses that were going up on Park Slope. With the houses on a single short block—Montgomery Place, just off Prospect Park—one developer produced a phantasmagoria of every Italianate, Romanesque, Queen Anne, and Renaissance style in the 1890s' architectural copybooks. The Litchfield family's railroad money had enabled them to build an Italianate villa on the

edge of what had since become Prospect Park, with a front yard *Willow Street,*
that reached almost to the harbor. Newer millionaires, such as *Brooklyn Heights*
members of Charles Pratt's family, built their sturdy homes on
Clinton Hill near Fort Greene, an area admired by Julian Ralph
for its croquet lawns. In Flatbush the last of the old Dutch farmhouses were being torn down to be replaced by planned subdivisions, such as Prospect Park South, where the streets would be
lined with imaginatively designed clapboard, shingle, and stucco
houses and the trees so arranged that every twenty feet a Norway

maple (for permanence) alternated with a Carolina poplar (for immediate shade).

As for old Brooklyn Heights, Ralph noted that the "district is not what it was in the days of yore." Many of the fine old brownstones were being turned into boarding houses or divided into small apartments, a trend that would continue until the late 1950s, when the Heights would be rediscovered by a new generation of the commuting Wall Streeters that Hezekiah Pierpont had advertised his lots to back in the 1820s. Seventy years after Ralph wrote about the "city of women," his own daughter died in a one-room, fifth-floor apartment of a once grand Heights brownstone. Like many of her neighbors, she was a widow who lived alone with her memories (which included having been one of Daniel Chester French's

OPPOSITE,
The Joseph Steele
Residence,
Lafayette Avenue
BELOW,
Clinton Avenue,
Clinton Hill

models for the sculptures on the New York Custom House at the foot of Broadway) and a worn collection of her father's magazine articles.

Once the bridge was open, the consolidation of Brooklyn and New York seemed inevitable. Within days of the opening ceremony James S. T. Stranahan addressed the New York Chamber of Commerce on the subject of geography. "The Thames," he pointed out, "flows through the heart of London and the Seine through the heart of Paris, but in neither case have you two cities. It is London on both sides of the Thames and Paris on both sides of the Seine." New York and Brooklyn, Stranahan believed, should profit from their example. "The people are the same people, have the same manners and customs, and have common commercial and social interests, and one municipal government would serve them quite as well as two, and at far less cost."

Money, not love, was always the argument for the match. Brooklyn believed it was morally superior to Manhattan, while Manhattan always regarded Brooklyn as a bit frumpish for its taste. The flirtation went on for nearly fifteen years—long enough for Brooklyn itself to consolidate with Flatbush and the rest of Kings County—until Manhattan finally asked for Brooklyn's hand (whereupon Brooklyn briefly, very briefly, affected coyness before finally saying yes). January 1, 1898, was the day Brooklyn became one of the five boroughs of Greater New York, an event that would be remembered by many Brooklynites as the Great Mistake.

It rained heavily on New Year's Eve 1897 as the crowds gathered at Brooklyn City Hall for a ceremony that was more a farewell to the City of Brooklyn than a welcome to the City of New York. The old hall was filled with ferns and cut flowers from the Prospect Park Conservatory, and hundreds of guests milled about, shaking hands with six former mayors, including Seth Low. There were no dress rules for the occasion, and some men were in formal dinner wear while others wore tweeds. The Society of Old Brooklynites, all wearing blue and gold badges, turned out en masse as they would have for the funeral of a fellow member. The mood, the *Eagle* reported, was one of "candid good nature slightly tinged with solemnity. . . . It could hardly have been said to be merry, but there was no trace of sadness." It was, in short, "a family gathering."

At nine o'clock as many as could squeeze in packed the Council *Fort Greene*
Chamber, with its rows of portraits of past mayors. After a silk
American flag was dipped in salute to the City of Brooklyn flag,
the mayor, Frederick Worster, spoke mournfully of the "passing
of this great city" and pointed out that "Brooklyn goes to New
York as anything but a penniless bride."

St. Clair McKelway, editor of the *Eagle* and principal speaker
of the evening, disagreed. "There need be no apology for the com-
parative poverty of Brooklyn," he said. "It is an honorable poverty
because the wealth Brooklyn has created . . . is represented in New
York. Brooklyn has become poor because of her contributions to
New York." The title of his talk was "Brooklyn for All—and All
for Brooklyn." McKelway was followed by Will Carleton, sometimes called the poet laureate of Michigan, who tried to lighten
things up a bit. He noted that if Manhattan was to be considered

the bridegroom and Brooklyn the bride, some notice had to be taken of Queens, the Bronx, and Staten Island. "Father Knickerbocker," he said, "may be in danger of indictment for polygamy." His poem for the evening, he explained, was written on the theory that there had been a death in the family, a comment that got the Society of Old Brooklynites applauding loudly. The poem concluded,

> This is not death; though a life link be broken,
> Still shall your sweet name forever be spoken.
> This is not death, but a second creation;
> Greater New York is your new incarnation!

The Old Brooklynites applauded that less enthusiastically.

Outside the rain had ended, and Seth Low, Mayor Worster, and a few others rushed over to the Brooklyn Bridge so that they could take the first train across after midnight. The sky to the west over New York City Hall at the other end of the bridge was bright with fireworks. The evening in Manhattan had been spent in celebration with trick bicycle riders, actors dressed up as Dutchmen and Indians, and demonstrations of fancy marching by an Irish drill team. At midnight New York time the mayor of San Francisco would press a button in California and the new flag of Greater New York would rise above City Hall. The consolidation of Greater New York was a national event.

North of the bridge a new East River suspension bridge was being built, the Williamsburg (with consolidation *Williamsburgh* would lose its *h*). Three new elevated train lines, from which Hugh McLaughlin's associates were said to have made a suspicious profit, now crisscrossed the city, and hundreds of acres of farmland in Gravesend and Flatlands were being divided into building lots because the new city taxes made farming impractical. With consolidation Brooklyn would be more of a city than ever.

At midnight the bell in the cupola of Brooklyn City Hall tolled the hour as the American flag was lowered and raised again with the Greater New York and Brooklyn flags. Factory whistles along the river began to blow and were answered by ships in the harbor and the shrill steam whistles of the elevated trains. Seth Low and his friends moved across the bridge toward Manhattan, where a hundred-gun salute pounded away in the night. Overhead a thousand skyrockets and Roman candles burned through the still-damp air. The Society of Old Brooklynites had already gone home. City Hall had become Borough Hall.

CHAPTER TWO
A City on an Archipelago

Hugging the southwest tip of Long Island, Brooklyn is part of a great archipelago that sits on the edge of the North American continent: Manhattan, Staten Island, Governors Island (once called Nut Island), Liberty Island (once Bedloe's), Roosevelt Island (formerly Welfare and before that Blackwell's), Ellis Island, and even—if you give a tiny, meandering creek more credit than it probably deserves—Coney Island.

The people of Brooklyn prefer to believe that they do not live on an island, and signs along the Belt Parkway and Brooklyn-Queens Expressway direct motorists eastward to Long Island as though they were not already there. North of the Newtown Creek and completely cutting off Brooklyn to the east is the Borough of Queens (where you go to catch an airplane or watch the Mets), and only beyond Queens, as far as Brooklyn is concerned, is really "the island." Three bridges and a tunnel under the harbor to Manhattan, eight subway connections, and a bridge to Staten Island all create the illusion that Brooklyn is part of the mainland. But with Newtown Creek, the East River, New York Harbor, the Atlantic Ocean, and Jamaica Bay, Brooklyn is actually surrounded on three sides by water.

On Brooklyn's northern border Newtown Creek, which shimmers with a sheen of OPEC green and blue, is about three miles long and at one time supposedly had more traffic on those three miles than the Mississippi River had on its nearly three thousand. Brooklyn's first oil refineries sprung up along its banks in the middle of the nineteenth century, and oil is still stored and transferred there. In fact, oil spills on the Newtown may have one of the longest pedigrees in the history of American industrial pollution. The creek is now the center of the Brooklyn-Queens scrap-iron business, and great heaps of rusted metal wait there to be taken to New Jersey.

Greenpoint forms the southern boundary of Newtown Creek, and if its waterfront warehouses look abandoned, as indeed many of them are, it still has its sugar and chemical plants. The shipyards that once employed twenty-five hundred workers are closed, and also gone is the porcelain factory that was best known locally not for its plates and vases but for its sandy river beach—which Greenpointers claimed had the best swimming in Brooklyn—and its piles of discarded, imperfect doorknobs, which were used as especially deadly "snowballs" in at least one memorable teenage gang battle.

From Greenpoint to the Williamsburg Bridge the riverside is lined with brick buildings that once housed breweries, sugar refineries, and flour mills. Now—no matter what the fading signs on the walls may say—they are warehouses or new homes of small businesses that left lower Manhattan in the mid-1970s when loft space there became more valuable as apartments than as factories or sweatshops for the garment industry.

To the south of the Williamsburg Bridge are the old Navy Yard, a Con Edison generating station that provides most of the power for the Wall Street area of Manhattan, and the Manhattan and Brooklyn bridges. Beyond the Brooklyn Bridge, stretching to Bay Ridge near the mouth of the Narrows, are the shipping piers: the Furman Street piers below the Brooklyn Heights bluff, the Red Hook piers, Atlantic Basin, Erie Basin, the Gowanus Canal, and the Northeast Marine, Bush, and Army terminals. The Furman Street piers were modernized in the 1950s just before the advent of container shipping, and most of the Brooklyn waterfront—except for 60 acres at Red Hook and 120 acres at Northeast Marine—is outfitted for "traditional" or "old-fashioned" break-bulk shipping. (The choice of terms depends on whether or not one is in the container business.) One container ship—in which the cargo is

Newtown Creek, with Queens and Manhattan in the distance

carried in prepacked aluminum and steel containers that are between twenty and forty feet long and eight feet wide and high—carries four to five times as much cargo as a break-bulk ship and is safer from pilferage because the goods are sealed into their containers.

In 1960, after southern ports began to prosper with container business, the New York longshoremen's union agreed to handle containers for an extra payment of a dollar a ton. The harbor accepted container ships for the first time, and the New York waterfront was never again quite the same. Today most of Manhattan's docks—those that haven't been torn down—stand empty, and even with about fourteen hundred ship dockings a year the Brooklyn piers are quiet. After the Civil War much of the overseas freight business had moved from South Street in Manhattan to more

Between the Navy Yard and the Manhattan Bridge

modern and cheaper piers in Brooklyn. A hundred years later there was another major move, this time to the other side of the harbor. Container shipping requires a great deal of storage space, and space is in short supply in Brooklyn. Port Elizabeth in New Jersey, with seemingly limitless amounts of empty swampland to turn into container storage space, now gets almost two thirds of the shipping business in New York Harbor.

After the piers stop at Bay Ridge, the Brooklyn waterfront becomes largely noncommercial. The old ferry slip at Sixty-ninth Street, which has been taken over by sunbathers, fishermen, and

A container ship unloads its cargo at Atlantic Basin in Red Hook

kids learning to ride new bicycles, marks the dividing line. Bay Ridge curves around to Fort Hamilton and the Verrazano-Narrows Bridge. Beyond is Gravesend Bay and the hook of Coney Island, where Sea Gate, which once considered itself the Palm Beach of New York and boasted Governor Smith as one of its favorite sons, still greets would-be visitors with the sign: "This Area Is Protected by Vicious Dogs. Do Not Enter—You Have Been Warned."

The boardwalk of Coney Island, where no one is warned away, leads to Russian-speaking Brighton Beach and Manhattan Beach and farther on to communities on Jamaica Bay, where high-rise "cities"—advertised by their developers as coming complete with schools, supermarkets, churches, synagogues, and health clubs (membership extra)—mix with bays of seemingly identical suburban houses whose owners' personalities are revealed not by their carefully clipped yards—also identical—but by the boats they have tied to the wooden docks in their backyards.

Tucked behind Manhattan Beach is Sheepshead Bay, a largely Irish-Italian community that likes to think of itself as a little fishing village or, perhaps, as the owner of a trendy seafood restaurant put it, as "the Sausalito of New York." Emmons Avenue, which runs along the bay, is lined with dozens of party boats, boats that every morning take out parties of sports fishermen. Most have signs telling what is biting (flounder, mackerel, porgies, blacks, or sea bass) and also list their departure times. Among the boats on a typical morning are the *Jet* ("7 A.M., Bait on Board"), *New Helen H.*, *Apache III*, *Amberjack V*, *Chief* ("Every Day: 10 A.M."), *Blue Sea III* ("Bottom Fishing, 7 A.M."), *Brooklyn V* ("6 A.M."), *Parable* ("8 A.M."), and for the landlubber at heart, the *Tampa VI* ("Featuring Air Conditioning, Lounge, Color TV, Heated Rails"). By 10:30 the Emmons Avenue pier is deserted.

In *Specimen Days*, Walt Whitman described the Brooklyn waterfront on a breezy June morning in 1878:

> . . . the mast-hemmed shores—the grand obelisk-like towers of the bridge, one on either side, in haze, yet plainly defined, giant brothers twin, throwing free, graceful, interlinking loops high across the tumbled tumultuous current below (the tide is just changing to its

Sea Gate

ebb)—the broad water-spread everywhere crowded—no, not crowded, but thick as stars in the sky—with all sorts and sizes of sail and steam vessels, plying ferryboats, arriving and departing coasters, great ocean Dons, iron-black, modern, magnificent in size and power, filled with

their incalculable value of human life and precious mer-
chandise—with here and there, above all, those daring,
careening things of grace and wonder, those white and
shaded swift-darting fish-birds (I wonder if shore or sea
elsewhere can outvie them), ever with their slanting
spars, and fierce, pure hawklike beauty and motion—
first-class New York sloop or schooner yachts, sailing this
fine day, the free sea in a good wind.

Whitman, who left Brooklyn during the Civil War, had returned
for a visit and spent the day sailing in the harbor and taking notes.
He added, "From my point of view, as I write amid the soft breeze,
with a sea temperature, surely nothing on earth of its kind can
go beyond this show."

One hundred and three years later, at six o'clock on another
breezy morning, the tugboat *New Jersey* backs slowly into the East
River from its berth below Brooklyn Heights and heads downstream toward Atlantic Basin, where a barge loaded with nine
empty freight cars waits to be hauled across the harbor to the New
Jersey railroad yards. The towers of the Brooklyn Bridge—which
was under construction that day Whitman went sailing—loom upstream out of the morning haze, and overhead the seagulls still
careen, but the harbor itself is empty. The only crowded place is
along the shore, where lines of trailer trucks, double-parked along
narrow Furman Street at the foot of the Heights, their engines

LEFT, *Mill Basin*
RIGHT,
*Shell Bank
Creek on
Sheepshead Bay*

idling, wait to get onto the Peruvian, Venezuelan, and Grancolombiana Line piers.

"These days Brooklyn gets the third-world ships," says the captain of the tug *New Jersey*, "from all the places that aren't modern enough for container shipping." From Brooklyn Bridge to Bay Ridge names on the piers form an odd gazetteer: Toro Lines, Djakarta Lloyd, Frota Amazonica, Maritime Company of the Philippines, South African Maritime, Saudi National Line, Yangming Transport, Hansa Line, Korea Shipping, Hellenic Lines, Jugolinija, Pakistan National Shipping, Compagnie Maritime Zairoise, Egyptian National, Turkish Cargo, Iran Express.

The *New Jersey* is one of four green-painted tugs—along with the *New York*, the *Brooklyn*, and the *Roy B. White*—in the New York Dock Railway fleet. The Dock Railway maintains about 35 miles of track scattered among five areas on Brooklyn's waterfront. It has 14 locomotives (not all of which are operational) and 31 railroad barges—called car floats—that the tugs use to haul freight cars from pier to pier and to the railhead at Greenville on the mainland in New Jersey.

The railway, which is probably unlike any other railroad in the country, owes its existence to the problems that arise out of trying to run a port on an island with limited rail connections to the mainland. Not only are the piers unconnected by rail, but also Brooklyn's only direct line to the nation's railroad system is roundabout, by a loop that crosses the Hudson just south of Albany (120 miles upriver), and low overpasses in the Bronx make *that* route impassable for many freight cars. By rail the only way west or south out of Brooklyn requires a trip by water across New York Harbor. The Dock Railway is the only outfit that makes the run.

It wasn't always that way. "Eight railroads used to have marine departments in the harbor," says the *New Jersey*'s captain, "with thirty-five crews each, and there were four small outfits like the Dock. At Greenville, which is the old Pennsy dock, one tug used to sit all day just to turn the floats around. When you blew your whistle to show you were going to back up, you had to be careful. There were so many boats around, people had trouble telling who was signaling. That was before we had radios. Now we signal and announce what we're doing over the radio, and there's no one around to run into if you tried."

The captain has been hauling car floats for twenty-eight years. Before that he spent three years as a deckhand, passing his pilot's test, and after a year as a mate passed his exam for a master's license. His father was a deep-sea diver on the island of Ischia, off Naples, and his children are in the advertising business in Manhattan. He lives, as he has most of his life, near Lady Moody's old cemetery in Gravesend.

"It's a good boat," he says about the *New Jersey*. "It was built in the early fifties in Oyster Bay for the New Haven Railroad. Thirteen hundred and fifty horsepower, a hundred feet long,

*End of the road
at Plum Beach*

twenty-seven wide. Working up here"—he gestures around the tongue-and-groove paneled pilot house—"is like having an eight-hour-a-day job on the top floor of a brownstone.

"On the docking tugs, we used to work with two full crews alternating six hours on, six off, two weeks on, two weeks off. You would come on duty for breakfast, and there would be white table-cloths, bacon, eggs cooked to order, cream of wheat, napkins, everything. Once a man got used to tugboats, he wasn't good for anything else. Barring sex, and you had to have a strong woman at home because half the time she was raising the family alone, it was a good life."

The *New Jersey* passes the foot of Atlantic Avenue and into Buttermilk Channel. Atlantic Avenue is the dividing line between the Heights and the lower-rent neighborhoods of South Brooklyn. One of the ferry lines once docked at its foot, and a huge glass factory also stood there until it moved upstate and changed its name to Corning. The avenue is the center of Brooklyn's Arab district, although many of the "Arabs" are actually Lebanese Christians, and amid the shish-kebab restaurants and antique shops are a few reminders of the neighborhood's waterfront past, such as the saloon that until a few years ago still had a small sign in its window: "Danish-Spanish Bar, Tables for Ladies."

Buttermilk Channel, which separates Brooklyn from Governors Island, was once shallow enough for cows to be herded across to graze on what was then called Nut Island. The channel may have received its name from the white water of its shallow rapids. At least one bear is on record for having attempted the same crossing. The *New York Gazette* of November 26, 1759, reported that a "large bear" wandered past the house of Cornelius Sebring in Red Hook and leaped into the channel. Mr. Sebring and a miller gave chase, both firing away with their muskets. The miller missed, but Sebring "sent the ball in at the back of his head, which came out of his eye, and killed him outright."

Since then the channel has been dredged to at least forty feet deep, and the shore of Governors Island is now lined with white Coast Guard vessels. The island has been in the hands of one branch of the military or another since before the Revolution. Colonel Jonathan Williams, Ben Franklin's grandnephew and the surveyor of Williamsburgh, designed for the island a fort which still stands, pointing its cannon toward Wall Street. The Army, Navy, and now the Coast Guard have all left their marks on the place, and as seen from Red Hook or from the pilot house of the *New Jersey* it is a tree-lined jumble of neofeudal fortifications, Victorian seaside villas, pseudo-Georgian apartment houses of the colonial style popular with college-dormitory architects of the 1950s, and what seems to be a Norman parish church.

The wind is stirring up whitecaps on Buttermilk Channel as the *New Jersey* turns into the narrow entrance of Atlantic Basin. On the left are the new cement piers of the Red Hook container port, and beyond them is a parking lot where the India Wharf Brewery once stood. As the tug pulls up alongside the waiting car float the *New Jersey*'s two hands and the mate come on deck to tie up to the barge. "They are my cowboys," says the captain. "They can hit anything with a line. Watch 'em. They never use a knot. One of them does the work of six Navy men." The mate signals the captain with a police whistle, and the captain reverses and advances the engines to tighten the lines. "It's like pitcher and catcher," he says. "We have to think with the same mind."

The *New Jersey* has a crew of five: a captain, a mate, two deckhands, and an engineer. There used to be also an oiler and a fireman, but the electric engine has made those jobs obsolete. All five live in Brooklyn or Staten Island. It is not a young crew. The engineer has been at it for forty years, and one of the deckhands—whose father was a tug captain—has been on the job for over thirty years. He rides to work every morning on a ten-speed bicycle that he keeps in the engine room. The mate is a refugee from one of Hitler's Polish death camps, and the kid—there's always a kid—is in his early thirties and balding. The kid on one of the other crews is black, but no women have yet cracked the ranks. "It's not a business," says the captain, "that sees a lot of new blood."

Women have managed to join the longshoremen's union, however. There are about eighty-three hundred registered longshoremen—the name's a nineteenth-century British contraction for men who work along the shore—employed in New York Harbor, and twenty-nine of them are women. In the boom days of the 1950s there were about twenty-two thousand longshore jobs to be had and about forty-eight thousand men available to fill them. Those were the days of the shape-ups made famous in movies such as *On the Waterfront*, when the available work gangs would line up every morning and the bosses—not always uninfluenced by payoffs—would choose who got the jobs. Traditionally Manhattan longshoremen were Irish (led by the Bradleys and the Gleasons), and those from Brooklyn were Italian (led by the Anastasios and the Scottos), but times are changing. The shape-up is no more; over a third of the longshoremen are now black; and the number of Brooklyn longshoremen is down to about thirty-five hundred.

Lashed to the float with its nine empty freight cars, the tug backs into Atlantic Basin and then out into Buttermilk Channel, where the high-riding, empty cars catch the wind. The float is 365 feet long and can carry as many as 18 railroad cars on its 3 tracks. "It's all a matter of balancing wind, tide, and weight," the captain explains. "The tide's always coming or going and can vary as much as four and a half feet. The sides of these boxcars act just like sails, and the wind can really play with them. The trick is to make nature work for you."

Turning out of the channel, the *New Jersey* passes Governors Island and heads westward across the harbor to New Jersey. The captain calls it the mainland, and he enjoys the fact that he sails past the Statue of Liberty and reaches the mainland of America four or five times a day and never sets foot on it. It's now 8:30, rush hour, and orange ferryboats are scattered between St. George on Staten Island and the Battery, but except for a few self-powered oil barges the harbor seems empty. "New York's always been an afternoon port," says the captain. An Italian fishing boat with *Palermo* painted across its stern is pulling into Erie Basin. "For spare parts or supplies," says the captain. "There are whole floating canneries out there, but they never come in unless someone runs out of olive oil or something." The glass buildings of lower Manhattan catch the morning sun, and as the tug moves across the harbor, for a split second the Statue of Liberty stands alone in the narrow space between the towers of the World Trade Center.

It all seems strangely unlike those crowded Currier & Ives lithographs of a harbor with every imaginable sort of craft packed gunwale to gunwale, or even unlike those old travel brochures of the mighty liners with their one, two, or three funnels passing through the lower harbor while fireboats and attending tugs huddle about. Even allowing for nineteenth and twentieth-century merchandising hype and the possibility that New York is indeed an

afternoon port, the harbor, and especially the East River, seem eerily quiet.

What's missing are the ferryboats. "There are fourteen ways to Brooklyn," a *Harper's Magazine* reporter wrote in the 1890s: 13 ferries and a bridge. The five major ferryboat lines to downtown Brooklyn alone accounted for 1,250 five-to-ten minute crossings a day, carrying 45,000,000 passengers a year. That equaled the population of the entire country, a Brooklyn booster of the 1880s pointed out.

If any Brooklynite was tempted to forget that he lived on an island, the ferry was there to remind him, and if ever he was to forget how much Brooklyn depended on Manhattan, the fact that the ferry franchises had to be leased from the city across the river was always a bitter reminder. The first ferry opened for business in 1642, when a Manhattan farmer and part-time saloonkeeper named Cornelis Dirckman established erratic service to Long Island by rowboat and sail at approximately the point where the

A Coast Guard patrol boat on the Gowanus Canal

A Bay Ridge inlet in the 1880s (LIHS)

Brooklyn Bridge now stands. This was a bit out of town, but it was where the river was narrowest, and Dirckman's inn was a convenient waiting room. It is quite likely that the saloon was a more profitable enterprise than the ferryboat, and until the end of the nineteenth century the ferry tavern was an important sideline of the ferry trade.

In 1654 ferryboats, like everything else in New Amsterdam, became regulated by Peter Stuyvesant, and hourly service was ensured from 5 A.M. to 8 P.M. in the summer (7 A.M. to 5 P.M. in winter), except when the Manhattan windmill "lowered its sail in consequence of storm." These early boats were small and dangerous—judging from the accident reports, most carried only about eight people and a horse or two—but with them Manhattan's control of the East River was established.

Under the British not only did Manhattan control the ferries, it claimed the entire river as its own and maintained that its "rights and privileges" extended to the high-water mark on Brooklyn's shore. It was a claim that stood up in court even after the Revolution, and until Brooklyn and Manhattan joined together in 1898, a Brooklyn commuter could stand at the Fulton ferry at low

"Steamboat Brooklyn *of the Fulton and South Ferry Company," by John and James Bard, twin brothers who painted portraits of nine boats in the Union Ferry Company fleet in the late 1840s.* (LIHS)

tide and see Manhattan mud at his feet. Even if a Brooklynite owned a boat, he could not use it to carry his own goods or cattle to market in New York. He was required to take the ferry.

The political possibilities of the ferry soon became apparent. In the 1690s a law was passed that forbade blacks to use ferryboats on the Sabbath unless their masters bought tickets in advance, which effectively kept free blacks from traveling on Sundays. During the Revolution the East River toll was raised by the Loyalists from a penny to an outlandish 6¢ (which the British military did not have to pay), putting a damper on civilian travel.

It was in 1814, though, that ferry service between New York and Brooklyn changed radically. In January of that year Robert Fulton, who with his steamboat and his friendship with the well-connected Livingston family had managed to win a monopoly on the use of steam engines on New York State waterways, announced the beginning of steam ferry service to Brooklyn. To pay for this modern wonder the fare would be raised from 2¢ to 4¢. Commuters were outraged. A town meeting was called, and Brooklyn's first committee to protest transit fares was organized. Petitions were signed and sent to the state legislature in Albany, but the result was the same as that of most transit protests since then. On May 1, when the steam ferry *Nassau* made its inaugural crossing, 549 passengers dutifully paid their 4¢ for the 12-minute trip. Serious commuters could subscribe $10 for a year-long "commutation" ticket, that seemingly quintessential twentieth-century suburban phenomenon.

The steam ferry's great rivals, also introduced in 1814, were the team boats, more often than not called horse boats because they were driven, literally, by horsepower—one to four teams of horses that would trudge around in tight circles, turning a drive shaft that turned the paddle wheels. Steam may have been a sign of progress, but for years commuters preferred the horse boats. They were just as fast and just as large, but they proved easier to navigate, steadier, and more reliable in foul weather.

But neither steam nor team was in fact all that reliable. When tides were strong or the river was clogged with ice, a trip that could take as little as four minutes might take up to an hour. Most boats had double hulls, rather like catamarans, with the paddle wheels mounted in the center. Foot passengers were on one side of the wheels, vehicles on the other. The engine rooms and cabins were one deck above—separate cabins for men and women, both equipped with coal stoves—and a deck above these was the pilot house, which was often completely open to the weather.

Walt Whitman, in "Crossing Brooklyn Ferry," saw the boats as a great symbol of the brotherhood of man:

> Just as you are refresh'd by the gladness of the river
>   and the bright flow, I was refresh'd,
> Just as you stand and lean on the rail, yet hurry with
>   the swift current, I stood yet was hurried,
> Just as you look on the numberless masts of ships and
>   the thick-stemm'd pipes of steamboats, I look'd.

An anonymous poet who frequented one of the Williamsburgh ferries was somewhat less lyrical. He wrote of "these leaky scows, stuffed with old rags/Well mixed with tar and feathers." He went on to describe them as:

Conveyances for man and brute
With filth up to the knees
Come on! Why don't you all commute
And take the ocean breeze?
Old "Noah's Ark" lies at the dock
Too rotten even to burn . . .
Her smoke-pipe how it stoops with age
All rusty and forlorn.

But ferries did burn. The old "Noah's Ark" of the poem was the *Noah Waterbury*, which escaped the fire at a Long Island terminal that destroyed or damaged several other ferries in 1853. During the same year a number of boats were lost as the result of collisions: a Catherine Street ferry rammed into the *Minnesota;* the *Keystone* hit the *Qualaska;* and the *Oneida* struck the *California.*

The Brooklyn ferries' moment of national glory came during the Civil War, when a half dozen or so boats were drafted into the Navy. They were painted black, mounted with heavy guns, and outfitted with a bit of protective armor. The men's cabins were turned into armories, and the women's became messrooms and sleeping quarters. As the *Commodore Perry* and the *Commodore Barney*, two boats from the Williamsburgh line sailed out of the harbor in 1861 to patrol the shoreline rivers of the Carolinas on

Captain's Pier at the foot of 20th Street on Gravesend Bay, 1922 (LIHS)

the lookout for privateers who had eluded the Union blockade of Southern ports. The *Perry* saw considerable action, and its list of victories included the capture of a boatload of bacon on the Roanoke River, while the *Barney* came home with an impressive war wound—a shot embedded in the side of the pilot house—and became something of a tourist attraction. Both boats went back into service after the war and plied the East River until 1890.

When Whitman wrote "Crossing Brooklyn Ferry" in 1856, an East River without ferryboats was incomprehensible:

> Fifty years hence, others will see them as they cross,
>   the sun half an hour high,
> A hundred years hence, or ever so many hundred years
>   hence, others will see them,
> Will enjoy the sunset, the pouring-in of the flood-tide,
>   the falling-back to the sea of the ebb-tide.

Fifty years hence the Brooklyn and Williamsburg bridges were carrying traffic, pedestrians, and trolley cars over the river. The Manhattan Bridge was then under construction, and the ferry business was doomed. The pattern was set years before, when the iron Penny Bridge (that was the toll) opened on Newtown Creek and put St. Patrick's Cathedral's special funeral ferryboat service out of business. With each new bridge more East River ferry lines shut down (and some of the boats themselves were sold off to see service as far away as Cuba), until 1940, when there was none. Brooklyn's last ferry, not on the East River but connecting Sixtyninth Street in Bay Ridge with Staten Island, closed after the Verrazano-Narrows Bridge opened in 1964.

The tug *New Jersey* drops off its car float of empty freight cars at the Greenville Yard between Jersey City and Bayonne, picks up a new low-riding float, and heads back across the harbor to the Bush Terminal in Brooklyn, now carrying a full load of nineteen boxcars. "We've carried everything," says the captain. "Lots of newsprint, for both the *Daily News* and the Jehovah's Witnesses, who print their *Watchtowers* in Brooklyn, flour, corn syrup, sewer pipes, lumber, lots of lumber, subway rails and ties, even whole subway cars. The next thing they want to get into is piggy-backing

trucks—just the trailers, not the cabs—from New Jersey to Bush Terminal to avoid the Manhattan bottleneck. So far it's been a lot of talk."

Looking up the hill to Sunset Park from Bush Terminal

Bush Terminal is a vast network of warehouses connected by the Dock Railway to deepwater piers. The *New Jersey* pulls into the terminal next to a Department of Sanitation Transfer Point— which is a rather nice way of describing an elevated pier from which garbage trucks dump their refuse into waiting scows. "The wind's against us," says the captain, sliding shut the pilot house windows. "When it's blowing the other way, the frogmen get it." On the other side of the sanitation pier are the docks of the police department's underwater rescue unit. It has been against the law to dump garbage in New York Harbor since the days of Sir Edmund Andros, the second British governor of the colony, and until the 1930s New York hauled its garbage out into the Atlantic and dumped it off the Jersey coast. Many people assume that is still going on when they see the loaded scows chugging out of Bush Terminal. Actually the boats are headed for Staten Island, where,

close to places with such lyric names as Fresh Kills, Island of *At Bush Terminal*
Meadows, and Cedar Point, the world's largest landfill project—
or dump—grows daily. Indeed, somewhere near the heart of Staten
Island will always be a good deal of Brooklyn.

At the pier a diesel locomotive is waiting for the *New Jersey* as
amid the blowing of police whistles the tug pushes the car float
up to a floating rail bridge. The locomotive moves slowly out onto
the bridge, its weight lowering the structure down deeper into the
water. When the railroad track on the bridge is aligned with the
track on the float, the deckhands hammer four yard-long metal
pins into place to hold them fast. "Just like putting together your
Lionel train track," says the captain. The tug drops its lines and
moves over to the other side of the pier, where it ties up to another
float and heads back to Greenville.

The last run of the day is to take a float load of tank cars from
Greenville up the East River to the Kent Avenue yard near the

Bushwick Inlet. "They're probably full of flour or baking soda or something like that," says the captain. "That's where the bakeries are." It is shortly after noon, and the tide is heading out as the *New Jersey* turns out of Buttermilk Channel into the East River, which, of course, is not a river at all, but a tidal estuary which connects New York Bay with Long Island Sound. The tug's top speed is about twelve knots, and it averages about eight, though with a heavy load going against a strong tide it is about half that. The boat passes the blue Furman Street piers and the old fireboat station near where the Fulton ferry once docked. A rebuilt coal barge has been turned into a music hall where chamber music and jazz concerts are performed, and next to it another barge, firmly grounded on dry land, is now a luxury restaurant that advertises its spectacular view of Manhattan rather than its food. Overhead, humming with traffic and wind soughing through its cables, is the Brooklyn Bridge.

"Through the bound cable strands, the arching path/Upward, veering with light, the flight of strings" is the way Hart Crane described this scene in *The Bridge*:

> Taut miles of shuttling moonlight syncopate
> The whispered rush, telepathy of wires.
> Up the index of night, granite and steel—
> Transparent meshes—fleckless the gleaming staves—
> Sibylline voices flicker, wavering stream
> As though a god were issue of the strings.

It is a special spot in the history of American literature, this place in the shadows of the granite foundations of the bridge. There is a small park here with the usual playground equipment and a row of old stone warehouses that now seem more important for the photographs Berenice Abbott and Walker Evans took of them than for any practical purpose they might have had. There's a parking lot, a number of newly renovated commercial buildings (one of which was once a plumbing fixtures manufacturer whose vivid toilet seat sign has unfortunately been removed in the spirit of good taste), and a wide expanse of patched cobblestone, probably made of old ship's ballast, where trailer trucks now wait at dawn. Overhead the fake crenelations of the Watchtower Society

proclaim Jehovah's kingdom. But this unlikely spot, at two very different times in its existence, inspired two of America's greatest poems, *The Bridge* and "Crossing Brooklyn Ferry." "Under thy shadow by the piers I waited," Hart Crane wrote, addressing the bridge. "Only in darkness is thy shadow clear."

The *New Jersey* labors on against the tide, and crossing under the Manhattan Bridge, it passes a shabby, forgotten-looking shed that bears a sign: BUILDERS OF THE WORLD'S MIGHTIEST WAR SHIPS. It is a relic of World War II, when the Brooklyn Navy Yard operated twenty-four hours a day, employing as many as seventy

Brooklyn Ferry, with the Brooklyn Daily Eagle *newspaper offices on the left, in the 1880s* (Stiles)

*The Eagle Warehouse
building, on the
site of the old
newspaper office*

thousand civilians to build, repair, and refit ships for the Navy.
The war years are remembered by one engineer who still works at
the yard as the first time women were employed to do more than
sew flags. The Navy Yard no longer exists. The federal government
abandoned it in 1966, all 265 acres of it, including 5 piers, 6 dry
docks, and nearly 40 buildings, some of which date back to the
first quarter of the nineteenth century.

There actually never was a Brooklyn Navy Yard. Its correct
title was the New York Naval Shipyard, and it came into opera-

ABOVE,
*The Brooklyn Navy
Yard in 1851*
(Gleason)
OPPOSITE,
The Bridge

tion in 1801, when John Adams's government bought a small ship-yard on Wallabout Bay and expanded it to build ships for the country's fledgling Navy. Adams was followed in the White House by Jefferson, whose embargo on foreign trade stranded nearly four hundred American ships in New York Harbor and left so many seamen out of work that the yard could employ three hundred men for no pay, just meals. A fine commandant's mansion, called Quarters A, was built in 1806. Charles Bullfinch, the architect of the Massachusetts State House, is sometimes given credit for its design, and it remains standing today without, its admirers like to point out, a single metal nail in its frame. The War of 1812 brought the Navy Yard into its own, and more than a hundred ships were armed and outfitted there, although the first ship actually built from the ground up, the *Ohio*, a seventy-four-gun ship of the line, was not launched until 1820.

The yard's first dry dock was completed in the 1840s, and if the Brooklyn Bridge is the harbor's engineering miracle of the second half of the nineteenth century, old Dry Dock Number One, still functioning, is the wonder of the first half. With its stepped granite sidewalls it looks today like an artifact from some earlier civilization, a Mayan ball court, perhaps, or a curiously inverted Egyptian

pyramid. Old Navy Yard hands like to claim that the *Monitor*, the Civil War ironclad, was built in Dry Dock Number One. Actually it was built according to John Ericsson's specifications at the Continental Iron Works in Greenpoint from steel plates forged at the Burdon Iron Works in upstate Troy and then taken to the yard to be outfitted. Everyone likes to take credit for the *Monitor*, with its round revolving turret, which enabled the guns to be aimed in any direction without having to maneuver the ship itself, but just as the yard often forgets to mention Greenpoint, Greenpoint usually ignores Troy's contribution.

Other, larger dry docks followed. Six thousand men worked in the yard during the Civil War, eighteen thousand during World War I. The *Maine*, later to be blown up in the Havana harbor, setting off the Spanish-American War, was built there, as were the battleships *Arizona* (sunk at Pearl Harbor) and *Missouri* (christened by Harry Truman's young daughter, Margaret, and eventually the site of the Japanese surrender) and the supercarrier *Franklin D. Roosevelt*. Built in 1945, the *FDR* was 963 feet long, only 37 feet shorter than the yard's longest dry dock.

For five years after the Navy left, the Navy Yard stood empty. The Officer's Club still functioned, a reserve ship on a training cruise would tie up from time to time, and the Navy kept its claim to Quarters A, but the dry docks began to sprout weeds. The roadways and piers began to crumble, and grass grew as high as the first-floor windowsills. In 1971 the federal government signed over most of the yard to the City of New York, and CLICK (the Commerce Labor Industry Corporation of Kings, Inc.) was formed to create jobs for the nearby communities of Bedford-Stuyvesant, Fort Greene, and Williamsburg by encouraging companies to rent space in the Navy Yard buildings. A shipbuilder used the old dry docks to build four supertankers—the *Brooklyn* (which squeezed under the bridge with four feet to spare), *Williamsburg*, *Bay Ridge*, and *Stuyvesant*, all good, solid Brooklyn names, even if *Stuyvesant* does mean "quicksand" in Dutch. But the company went bankrupt amid a flurry of investigations by the district attorney's office, and now, except for ship repair work done for the Navy by Coastal Dry Dock, CLICK renters make little or no use of the waterfront.

About forty companies rent out space in the various buildings, operations that range from a one-man furniture maker to a hand-

bag factory to a liquor warehouse to a company that distributes sugar substitutes to a glass-and-mirror works to a working forge. And for a nice swords-into-plowshares touch a pewter factory housed in a former naval armaments building made the chalice Pope John Paul II used when he celebrated Mass on the Washington, D.C., mall in 1979.

Nearly three thousand workers are employed by the CLICK companies, all neighborhood people, 85 percent of them black or Puerto Rican. "There's a huge labor force here," says the president of CLICK, an industrial engineer who was born in Red Hook, "but it is untrained. When the yard was the Navy Yard, there was an active apprentice program. Kids were learning how to become mechanics or electricians. When the yard closed, all those people left and a whole tradition was lost. Our renters know we have the manpower available. It just has to be trained. And they like us for our security. All the old Navy security is still in place. The yard's a fortress. Our renters want to be near the work force, but I think they are a little afraid of them, too." CLICK recently changed its name to the Brooklyn Navy Yard Development Corporation.

Beyond the Navy Yard the *New Jersey* meets her sister boat the *New York* coming downstream from Newtown Creek. It is dragging two barge loads of scrap metal, one on either side, that will

A working forge in a commercial metal shop at the Navy Yard

be added to the Greenville scrap piles on the mainland. Beyond the Williamsburg Bridge is the old Havemeyer and Elders' sugar mill, where the Dock Railway began after the turn of the century as a branch of the company's cooperage department. A way was needed to move the heavy barrels, and a small railway seemed an easy solution. Close by is an abandoned brewery, its brick sides ripped open like those of an egg carton so the valuable copper vats could be taken to newer operations in another city. Of the dozens of breweries that used to be located in Brooklyn, all have closed or moved away, including one that still advertises that it and "this town practically grew up together."

Farther upstream, skirting the Williamsburg shore, where family hotels once did a brisk business catering to people who wanted to enjoy the water without traveling as far as Coney Island (and where hotels not so family oriented offered secluded hideaways just a ferry ride from Manhattan), the *New Jersey* turns slowly against the current into the dock of the old Eastern District Railway Yard. The narrow rail yard extends from the crowded dock through the streets of the neighborhood, which was once famous for its bakeries and breweries. Commercial baking is still done there, and the smell of hot dough mixes with the oily tang of the river.

It is the last stop of the day, and everyone moves quickly. The deckhands secure the car float and jump back aboard the tug. The police whistle blows for a last time, and the *New Jersey* signals and backs out into the river, catching the tide, and, free from the cumbersome restraint of a barge, races with the river toward its home pier. The mate is now at the wheel, the captain having gone below to change from his work clothes—a Basque beret, corduroys, a Pendleton shirt, and a sweater—to a yellow Ban-lon shirt and gray wash pants. He keeps to the Manhattan side of the river and passes a fireboat station. ("The easiest job on the waterfront," he says. "All they do is keep their boat clean.") As the tug passes under the Brooklyn Bridge the captain again takes over, cuts the power, and pulls the *New Jersey* into its berth directly behind the tug *Brooklyn*.

By the time he locks the pilot-house door with its civil defense poster giving instructions on how to clear the harbor in case of atomic attack, the crew has tied up the boat and are heading for their cars. The engineer has killed the electric engine. The deckhand with the ten-speed bike is already out the gate. Overhead traffic can be heard moving along the Brooklyn-Queens Expressway. Cantilevered above is the promenade of Brooklyn Heights, where someone with a camera, probably a tourist, is leaning over the railing to take a picture of the Manhattan skyline. It is about two o'clock, and indeed, the afternoon port is busier, mostly with tankers bearing oil company insignia.

"The one thing I haven't mentioned," says the captain, "is how beautiful this job is, the sights I get to see, the fog, rainbows. You wouldn't believe the colors."

Henry James, too, was struck by the sometimes puzzling beauty of the port. In 1904, toward the end of his life, James made a return visit to New York and, like Whitman on his visit twenty-six years before, spent part of a day in the harbor. With typical Jamesian precision—and rather atypical enthusiasm—he tried, in his *The American Scene*, to analyze the beauty of the place:

> It is indubitably a "great" bay, a great harbour, but no one item of the romantic, or even of the picturesque, as commonly understood, contributes to its effect. The shores are low and for the most part depressingly furnished and prosaically peopled; the islands, though numerous, have not a grace to exhibit, and one thinks of the other, the real flowers of geography in this order, of Naples, of Capetown, of Sydney, of Seattle, of San Francisco, of Rio, asking how if *they* justify a reputation, New York should seem to justify one. . . . There is a beauty of light and air, the great scale of space, and, seen far away to the west, the open gates of the Hudson. . . . But the real appeal, unmistakably, is in that note of vehemence in the local life . . . for it is the appeal of a particular type of dauntless power. The aspect the power wears then is indescribable; it is the power of the most extravagant of cities, rejoicing, as with the voice of the morning, in its might, its fortune, its unsurpassable conditions, and imparting to every object and element, to the motion and expression of every floating, hurrying, panting thing, to the throb of ferries and tugs, to the plash of waves and the play of winds and the glint of lights and the shrill of whistles and the quality and authority of breeze-born

cries . . . something of its sharp free accent. . . . The im-
measurable bridges are but the horizontal sheaths of
pistons working at high pressure, day and night, and
subject, one apprehends with perhaps inconsistent gloom,
to certain, to fantastic, to merciless multiplication.

Out beyond the newest bridge, the Verrazano-Narrows, the fishing boats are returning to Sheepshead Bay, followed by plumes of
gulls fighting for the discarded guts of the newly cleaned fish. The
boats return in single file, coming around Breezy Point at the end
of the Rockaways, crossing the inlet past Manhattan Beach and
Oriental Beach, where the new community college is located, and
entering the narrow bay.

In spite of the fleet there are no commercial fishermen in Sheepshead Bay, and the fish at most of the seafood restaurants that line
Emmons Avenue on the waterfront come from elsewhere. The local
sea bass, says one of the restaurant owners, smells of kerosene.
The bass she serves comes from Virginia, and red snapper from
Florida. The fishermen who pay to go on the boats are there for
the fun of it—for the fishing and the now-empty coolers of beer
they drag ashore—and many of them don't even claim the fish
they've caught, leaving them for the crews to deal with. So along
Emmons Avenue and on the boat docks crewmen sit with buckets
of porgies or mackerel or flounder, and local housewives and shop-
pers from other neighborhoods come by to bargain.

Every afternoon, when the weather is nice, a small crowd
gathers to watch the boats return, just as fishermen's wives might
gather on the beach of a real fishing village. But these are men,
in their sixties or older, in sporty plaid trousers, matching white
shoes and belts, and Irish rain hats. They live in the retirement
homes and hotels that have sprung up near the bay, and as the
afternoons lengthen and the boats come chugging around the point
they get dressed up and come down to the water to watch the
boats, compare the catches, and gossip. Herman Melville once
wrote of the "crowds of water-gazers," landsmen all, who filled
the East River piers on Sunday afternoons. Here are their descendants, on a paved-over spit of sand on a narrow inlet on a long
island, gazing seaward as the sun sets in the great harbor that is
out of sight behind them.

ABOVE LEFT,
*Ship repair yards
on Erie Basin*
BELOW LEFT,
*Sheepshead Bay,
with Manhattan
Beach in the
foreground and
Emmons Avenue
running across
the top of the
picture*

CHAPTER THREE
A City of Open Spaces

Brooklyn didn't have many landmarks in 1776, but early on an August morning of that year young militiamen from New England destroyed one of them, the huge white oak that marked the rural boundary between the villages of Brooklyn and Flatbush. The tree stood at the foot of Valley Grove Pass on the only road between the towns. The troops hoped to halt the British advance on New York City, and the oak, along with other trees, was chopped down. The road and the pass through the hills were blocked. If the British and their Hessian mercenaries weren't stopped, they would at least be slowed down by the chaos. A Pennsylvania volunteer who fought at the pass later recalled soldiers "crying out to their fellows for God's sake to help them out, but everyman was intent on his own safety and no assistance was rendered."

On Prospect Park maps Valley Grove Pass is now called Battle Pass, and the site where the white oak stood, just beyond the zoo, at the point where out-of-condition bicyclists dismount to push their bikes to the top of the hill, is commemorated with a historical marker (or was, until someone managed to unbolt the bronze tablet and patriotic eagle and cart them away). At least one Bicentennial guidebook recommended a visit, claiming it was the only metropolitan battlefield that had remained unchanged since 1776. It hasn't, of course. A little over a century ago the pass became part of a magnificent stage set, a five-hundred-and-twenty-six-acre park created between 1866 and 1874 by Frederick Law Olmsted and Calvert Vaux, the architects of Manhattan's Central Park.

Shaped like a chipped arrowhead aimed toward Manhattan, Prospect Park has three distinct topographies: a broad, rolling meadow that curves through seventy-five acres; wooded hills; and a "lake district" featuring—as park officials described it in 1866—"a fine sheet of water, with picturesque shores and islands." To create this natural-looking setting, Olmsted and Vaux drained swamps, filled glacial kettle holes, moved fully grown trees, and tore down houses (including a country inn at Battle Pass). They blasted out rocks to create meandering streams, hauled boulders to form waterfalls, and imported shrubbery from all over the world to cover the "wild" hills.

It was not a park for flowers, the partners said, but a park for dramatic landscapes with room for "several thousand little family and neighborly parties to bivouac at frequent intervals through the summer." The lake they built, which was planned as much for winter ice skating as for summer boating, filled sixty acres, twice the size of their Central Park lake. Operation of the idyllic lake district, where water flowed from ponds through rocky streams and over waterfalls to the tranquil Lullwater and then on to the lake, required the services of a massive steam boiler and pump—tastefully hidden away behind a mock-Tudor doorway—that could churn seven hundred fifty thousand gallons of water a day. Around the edges of the park they constructed a chain of rolling hills to blot out all sight of the city that would grow up around it, a secluding touch they had not used when building rectangular Central Park.

The park was planned to be seen at its best from its carriage roads, and an area was set aside near Music Island—now the site of the ice-skating rink—where people could park and listen to concerts without having to leave their carriages, a precursor, perhaps, of the drive-in movie theater. The park was also laid out so that pedestrians entered it through a series of romantic tunnels and underpasses without ever having to cross roads and encounter traffic. For all its natural veneer Prospect was designed along very modern lines.

Prospect Park's wooded hills

ABOVE, *Surveying Prospect Park, ca. 1865. The two men holding the map have been identified, without overwhelming evidence, as Calvert Vaux (left) and Frederick Law Olmsted (right).* (LIHS) BELOW, *Flatbush, as seen across the new lake in Prospect Park, in 1869* (LIHS)

When Olmsted and Vaux accepted the Central Park commission in 1857, it came with two chunks of land carved out for use as museum sites. They made sure the same mistake wasn't made in Brooklyn. The original plan for the park included land on both sides of Flatbush Avenue. The partners rejected the land on the eastern side of Flatbush and suggested that it be set aside for museums and "other educational edifices," thereby saving their park from intrusion. (Today the Brooklyn Museum, Public Library, and Botanic Garden stand there.) The fact that they didn't want museums on park land, however, did not mean they were against buildings. They built a small menagerie and a dairy, complete with a resident farmer, where costumed milkmaids sold cold glasses of milk from park cows. There were public restrooms, carefully hidden from sight, several rustic shelters, a sheepfold, and a bandstand, all designed to fit into the park ambiance, which Olmsted described as "rural, natural, tranquillizing and poetic." Later, from other hands, would come Italianate boathouses and croquet shelters, greenhouses, concrete band shells, a merry-go-round, children's playgrounds, a distinctly untranquillizing and unpoetic skating rink with artificial ice (when Brooklyn winters turned too warm to freeze the lake), a full-sized replica of Mount Vernon (erected by Sears, Roebuck in honor of George Washington's two hundredth birthday and torn down a year later), and a red brick zoo built in the 1930s by the WPA on the site of Olmsted and Vaux's deer paddock. It may say something about the spirit of the zoo that for years its most popular exhibit was a vulture.

In Prospect Park, Brooklyn had the finest, most expertly designed urban park in the country, a park noticeably superior—as any Brooklynite could tell you—to Central Park. Rivalry with New York was an important factor in the park movement in Brooklyn from its very beginning. In the 1820s, when Brooklyn was in the midst of its first real estate boom, voices began to be raised to set aside land for public use. The first cry, though, was not for a park but for a cemetery. "It should be an object of admiration," an advocate wrote to the *Long Island Star* in 1825, "not only to ourselves, but more so to strangers." (For "strangers," read Manhattanites.)

A year later a proposal for a traditional park came from Hezekiah Pierpont, the Heights real estate promoter, who suggested

ABOVE,
Prospect Park Lake
LEFT,
Cross-country
skiing on the
Long Meadow
RIGHT,
Picnicking at the
Concert Grove
Lagoon in 1897
(LIHS)

that a public promenade a hundred and fifty feet wide be established along the Heights so that the harbor view and breezes might be enjoyed by all. A few cynics pointed out that the promenade, outside of whatever good it might provide the commonweal, would protect Pierpont's building lots from being cut off from those same breezes. If people wanted to enjoy the view, they argued, they could go to the Colonnade Gardens, an outdoor restaurant just below the edge of the Heights. Someone, perhaps none too seriously, later suggested that a promenade be built along the roofs of the houses on the Heights.

Pierpont did have one important and energetic supporter in Alden Spooner, editor of the *Long Island Star*. In an editorial Spooner pointed across the harbor to the new park New York had built on the Battery. "Unless we can get a part of these Heights ensured to us [for public use]," he wrote, "New York will ever possess a claim of what we shall forever be deprived." He had struck home. New York had a park, a popular park where all the

best people went to be seen, while Brooklyn had nothing. But there were finally too many objections to Pierpont and his Heights proposal—it wouldn't be until 1951 that Pierpont's promenade came into existence, an unexpected bonus of Robert Moses's Brooklyn-Queens Expressway—but attention turned to a bothersome swamp on Wallabout Bay.

Why not haul dirt from a nearby hill, where remains of old Fort Greene and War of 1812 entrenchments could still be seen, and dump it in the Wallabout swamp? That way a useless hill would be leveled—a pleasing idea to builders and developers, who saw the area in terms of building lots—and a vile swamp could be turned into a park. In 1835 Brooklyn began work on its first landfill project.

Spooner couldn't have been happier. Without a park, he had written in the *Star*, Brooklyn was "a house without windows . . . a man without nostrils." In "nostrils" he had hit upon an unfortunate word, for before long anyone with a nose knew the landfill park was a disaster. When it was dumped into the swamp, the dirt from Fort Greene had turned into a huge mud pie—a smelly, insect-infested mud pie. It wasn't until the mid-1840s that the mud finally solidified. City Park had by then cost almost $100,000, the most expensive public project in Brooklyn until then. Now high and dry and even outfitted with a modern swimming pool, the former mudhole is called Commodore John Barry Park.

Although Walt Whitman, then editor of the *Brooklyn Daily Eagle*, called the landfill park "a miserable piece of a place," he was not against parks in general. "The greatest loveliness of Brooklyn," he wrote in the *Eagle*, "consists in the plentifulness of its trees—those tokens of nature's freshness. . . . The more we have of them the better." The ideal spot for a park, he thought, was not the Wallabout swamp or the Heights, but the old Fort Greene hill, which had only been dented by the landfill project. It was higher than the Heights, had a better view of the harbor, and had valid historical associations. Best of all it was in the middle of the part of town where "the swarmingness of population," as he phrased it, was thickest. As for the often repeated objection that the neighborhood was "too Irish" to justify the city's investing in another expensive park, Whitman proclaimed it to be the home of "the mechanics and artificers of our city," whose "neat plain homes"

Hezekiah Pierpont's proposed Brooklyn Heights promenade was finally realized with the building of the Brooklyn-Queens Expressway in the 1950s.

were "without ornamental attraction, except for their children." It was also, incidentally, the part of town where Whitman lived.

The park was built. It opened on Thanksgiving Day in 1848 as Washington Park, although everyone called it Fort Greene, and later its name was changed to that. Spooner of the *Star* declared it "worth as much local rejoicing as our victories in Mexico." The neighborhood agreed. Unlike the swampy field a few blocks away, the thirty-acre hillside park could be used and enjoyed. In fact, it was used so well that by the following spring indignant letters began appearing in the newspapers complaining that the mechanics and artificers were allowing their pigs to run unattended in the new park and that someone had taken away "cart loads" of the new green sod.

Fort Greene Park and the memorial to the prison ship martyrs

But there was always something starkly ceremonial about Fort Greene. It was a place for Fourth of July speeches and memorial observances, a place where troops were massed and addressed before being sent off to war. In 1860 Olmsted and Vaux had circled the hill with steps, plazas, and concentric paths, and in 1908 the architectural firm of McKim, Mead, & White topped it off with what was proclaimed the world's tallest Doric column (148 feet 8 inches) to mark the new burial place of the thousands of men who died on the prison hulks of Wallabout Bay.

There is a nice irony there. One of the reasons Whitman had advocated a park on the Fort Greene hill was his hope that the prison ship martyrs would be buried there. In 1808 Tammany Hall had staged an elaborate ceremony during which the prisoners' bones were placed in a temporary vault near the Navy Yard. The procession featured a black horse with trailing black plumes bearing a black-clad rider who carried a black silk banner that read: "Mortals avaunt! 11,500 spirits of the murdered brave approach the tomb of honor, of glory, and of virtuous patriotism!" Over the years the tomb had fallen into disrepair, and Whitman, on whatever newspaper he worked, waged an almost continuous campaign to do something about that. In his 1861 "Brooklyniana" column in the *Standard* he commented that if indeed the park became the new burial site, "we hope it will not be spoilt by adopting any such absurd designs as by some adverse fates have fixed upon all other American monuments . . . even the chimney-shaped Bunker Hill monument in Boston." Today, Whitman might not be surprised to note, the world's tallest Doric column looks like a very elegant chimney, and it is capped with a huge bronze brazier which once contained an eternal flame. It has long since gone out.

The greatest boon to Brooklyn parkland was, oddly enough, a charter that allowed for the establishment of a privately owned cemetery on a ridge overlooking New York Harbor not far from the Narrows. Necropolis was the first name considered for the place, but the developers rejected it in favor of the more cheerful-sounding Green-Wood, and until the opening of Prospect Park it remained the most popular outdoor gathering place—and picnicking spot—in Brooklyn. In 1866, after the cemetery had become well established, *The New York Times* wrote, "It is one of the institutions to be served up to all strangers, and no guest has been courteously entertained until he has been driven through its winding avenues and looked down on the city from its commanding heights. It is the ambition of the New Yorker to live upon 5th Avenue, to take his airings in [Central] Park, and to sleep with his fathers in Greenwood." The *Times* made *Green-Wood* into one word, and so, from the beginning right up to the current subway map, has just about everyone else.

The cemetery was the dream of another Pierpont, Hezekiah's son, Henry, who had changed the spelling of the family name to the more Frenchified Pierrepont. He had been greatly impressed with Mount Auburn, the "rural" cemetery across the river from Boston in Cambridge, which had opened in 1831 and become an instant social success. With the rapid crowding of Brooklyn and Manhattan, he believed, a New York rural cemetery was also assured of popularity. But the cemetery remained only a dream until Pierrepont joined forces with David Bates Douglass, a designer of canals, bridges, and aqueducts. Under Douglass's guidance the cemetery was chartered in 1839 as a nonprofit organization with $300,000 in capital and the right to purchase 200 acres. Mount Auburn had only 72 acres, Pierrepont was quick to point out. Before it was finished, Green-Wood would have 478.

For the design of his new cemetery Douglass took his cue both from Mount Auburn and from the ideas of the popular Hudson Valley landscape architect Andrew Jackson Downing, whose aim in gardening was to achieve "a certain spirited irregularity." Green-Wood's roads and paths wind through wooded lanes and narrow valleys. There are ponds, small streams, and artfully molded hills, and—since the cemetery is on the highest point of land in Brooklyn—frequent views of the harbor. Richard Upjohn was commissioned to design a grand ceremonial gateway that would celebrate in red sandstone three resurrections from the Bible, those of Jesus, Lazarus, and the widow's son. To comfort visitors who expected a more permanent interment, the gateway also pictured allegorical scenes of Faith, Hope, Memory, and Love. Towering over the spiked archways is a steeple containing a bell that still tolls as funeral corteges approach. An 1867 guidebook commented approvingly that the Gothic design was "not only religious but Christian."

Manhattan tourists could get to Green-Wood by taking a ferry

from the Battery to the Hamilton Avenue slip, where carriage tours could be arranged at the cost of 25¢ for adults, 10¢ for children. Stops on the tour included graves of the famous (Currier, Ives, De Witt Clinton, Horace Greeley, Lola Montez, Henry Ward Beecher) and the rich (William Niblo, the theater owner who donated the goldfish in Green-Wood's ponds, and John Matthews, the inventor of carbonated water) and various historical monuments (to the men who died in the Battle of Long Island, to the victims of a theater fire, to the city's firemen). But there were also curiosities: for instance, the grave of Dixon H. Lewis, a congressman from Alabama who was famous for requiring two chairs to support his considerable girth when he sat in the House of Representatives. To answer the obvious question, a guidebook noted, "He is buried here due to the fact that he happened to die in New

Richard Upjohn's Green-Wood Cemetery gate (Stiles)

York." Such burials of convenience were one of the regular services of nineteenth century cemeteries. Charles Dickens, who visited a New York cemetery, possibly Green-Wood, in 1842, described it as suburban, spacious, and unfinished, "yet, everyday improving" and added, "the saddest tomb I saw there was 'The Strangers' Grave.' Dedicated to the different hotels in the city."

The tour-book writers made no attempt to hide their feelings about the different tombs. G. K. Garrison's white marble oriental vault, which looks something like a giant stone tent, was universally admired: "Much care has been taken to give the entire a solid and effective character, at a great outlay of money." But outlay of money was not always enough. The grave of the wife of the painter George Catlin (located near the junction of Landscape Avenue, Aspin Hill, and Sylvan Bluff, a typically lyrical Green-Wood intersection) featured "a winged female form inscribing a final message." Nehemiah Cleaveland, in his 1867 guide, says flatly, "This work of somewhat questionable taste was executed in France."

Another controversial stone was that of "C. Griffith." It shows Mr. Griffith saying farewell to his wife in front of their brownstone house while, waiting in the distance, stands a horse-driven Sixth Avenue streetcar, raising the troubling possibility that death, which traditionally rode a white horse, was now traveling by modern horsecar. John Matthews, the father of the modern soda fountain, also came into criticism for the "Hindoo Temple" in which he lay—in sculpture—wrapped in a winding sheet, protected by four fierce mythological beasts. It reflected, sniffed Effie Brower in her lachrymose *Greenwood Leaves*, "the hideousness of a morbid taste." A more lively "special attraction," as Cleaveland phrased it, was Captain John Correja, both the captain himself and the life-sized statue of him standing sextant in hand. "As long as his strength permitted," Cleaveland wrote, "he came often to see it; kept everything in order; and listened with evident complacence to the remarks of wondering and admiring strangers."

Everyone's favorite grave, the stop without which no tour was complete, was "The French Lady's Monument." It was the tomb of Charlotte Canda, the daughter of a French schoolmaster who claimed to have been an officer of Napoleon's. She was killed in a carriage accident on the evening of her seventeenth birthday. The

ABOVE LEFT,
*Along
Amarylis Path*
ABOVE RIGHT,
Captain Correja
BELOW LEFT,
*Mr. Griffith says
farewell*
BELOW RIGHT,
*A detail from
Matthews's
"Hindoo Temple"*

monument, a filigree Gothic altar with a statue of a madonna, was designed by Charlotte herself. (The madonna's face was believed to have been modeled on Charlotte's, but—said John Mountain in his guide—it was only a tolerable likeness.) A beautiful, exotic, artistic girl cut off at the very moment of her blooming, Charlotte was everything a romantic Victorian could want to find in a cemetery. Her grave was even more popular, said one loyal guidebook, than the most popular tomb at Mount Auburn—which also happened to be that of a young girl.

So the crowds arrived. The *Long Island Star* clocked in a hundred and eighty carriages on one June Sunday in 1845, years before Green-Wood hit its stride as a tourist attraction. The cemetery became so concerned about its public image that it published a book of "hints" on proper burial ground etiquette for plot owners. Children's graves should not be decorated with toys, it chided, and "as to the artificial flowers, they belong to Canal-street." Most of all the cemetery pleaded for decorum: "Fond mourner—confine your passionate utterances to the friendly bosoms that share your grief; or, still better, breathe them only in your secret sighs."

Plots sold briskly at a hundred dollars, or four or more for

Greek temples
on Vine Avenue

eighty-five dollars each, and the success of the place won Douglass commissions to design cemeteries in Albany and Quebec, as well as the presidency of Kenyon College. The people of Brooklyn, with their picnics and carriage rides, had turned Green-Wood—far more than Fort Greene—into the kind of park they wanted. But no matter how large or picturesque, a cemetery could never take the place of a park. It was an attempt to match Green-Wood's view of the harbor and its rolling, wooded landscape that drew the park commissioners' attention to Mount Prospect, the second highest point in Brooklyn.

Mount Prospect—located behind the present site of the Public Library on Grand Army Plaza—was the site of the city reservoir, and the commissioners had for years been buying up land around it with vague plans of creating a Mount Prospect Park to rival Manhattan's newly announced Central Park. As the plan passed through the hands of various architects before ending up with Olmsted and Vaux, the shape of the plot changed, and by 1866, when work began, the "Mount" had been dropped from the park's name and Mount Prospect itself stood outside the park's boundaries.

A park philosophy had also evolved—two philosophies really, which had the good fortune to mesh together nicely. James S. T. Stranahan—the president of the Parks Commission and the man Henry Stiles, the city's official nineteenth-century historian, called Brooklyn's Baron Haussmann (after the city planner who rebuilt Paris for Napoleon III)—saw the parks as a political force. They

were a way of unifying all of Kings County into the City of Brooklyn, which was but one step in his plan to make Brooklyn the most
influential borough of a mammoth City of New York.

For Olmsted and Vaux a parks system was not only a pleasant
adornment to city life but also a city service as important, and as
functional, as the sewer system. The hope of the future lay in the
cities, Olmsted believed, but he also saw them as dangerous places.
City people tended "to regard others in a hard if not always hard-
ening way." The very air they breathed was harmful. Olmsted
wrote to the park commissioners: "With every respiration of every
living being a quantity is formed of a certain gas, which, if not
dissipated, renders the air of any locality at first debilitating, after
a time sickening and at last deadly." The solution to these mental
and physical problems was ample park space. "A great object of
all that is done in a park, of all the art of a park," he wrote, "is to
influence the mind of men through their imagination." Open spaces
in parks, Olmsted argued, gave city dwellers the freedom to be
less watchful and more gregarious, more—to use his word—
"neighborly," while the park trees and plants purified the air they
breathed. His suggestion for a way to spread the advantages of
parklike conditions throughout the city was to build—and this was
perhaps the first time the word was used—"parkways," wide avenues, planted down the center with trees and shrubs, that would
radiate out of Prospect Park. Eastern Parkway—the tree-lined
boulevard that begins today at the Grand Army Plaza park entrance and passes the Brooklyn Museum, countless West Indian
goat-meat sandwich counters, and the world headquarters of a
Hasidic sect before ending amid the burnt-out tenements of East
New York—was laid out by Olmsted and Vaux, as was Ocean
Parkway, which was intended to connect the park with Coney
Island.

A tradition of park building had been firmly established, and for
the rest of the century, often on Olmsted's advice, the city set aside
"picturesque places for public recreation." They stretch across the
width of Brooklyn, from Dyker Beach Park on Gravesend Bay
(now largely taken up by a golf course) to Tompkins Park in
Bedford-Stuyvesant to Greenpoint's Winthrop Park. (Now called
Monsignor McGoldrick Park, the latter is dominated by a statue of
a naked sailor pulling on a hawser, a muscular memorial to the
designer of the *Monitor*.)

Grand Army Plaza,
with the Soldiers'
and Sailors'
Memorial Arch

With the Botanic Garden, which opened in 1910 across Flatbush Avenue from Prospect Park, Brooklyn finally had a park that was designed for the display of flowers, fifty acres of rock gardens and daffodil hills, water-lily pools, a children's garden, a fragrance garden for the blind (with labels in braille), stands of bamboo, a terrace of topiary beasts, and sections of azaleas, dogwoods, for-

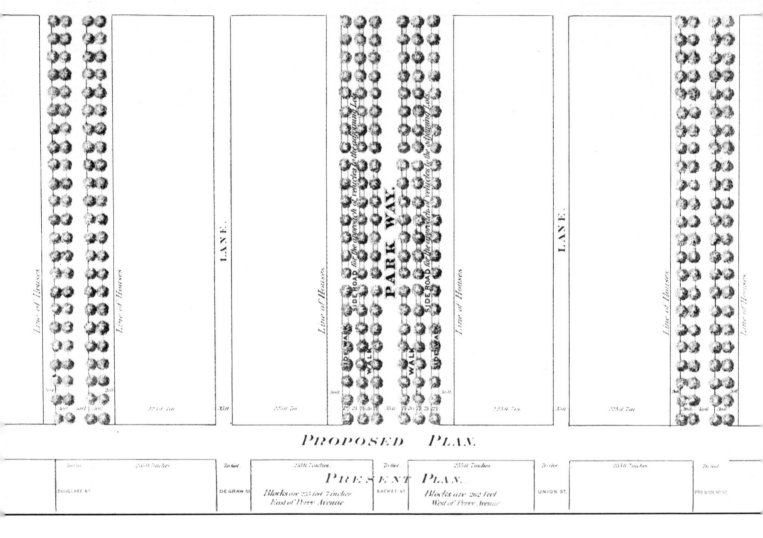

sythia (Brooklyn's official flower), and rhododendron. The rose garden (five thousand bushes, nine hundred varieties) is popular, but the big crowd pleaser comes every spring when the Japanese cherry trees bloom. Each Brooklyn cherry blossom is double, unlike the single variety that blooms in Washington, D.C., and every

OPPOSITE,
*The original
Park Way plan
submitted by
Olmsted and Vaux
in 1868* (PC)
LEFT,
*Eastern Parkway
today as it
passes the dome
of the
Brooklyn Museum*

year the grass beneath the long paired corridors of cherry trees is crowded with flower lovers, lovers, baby carriages, strolling couples, and even entire wedding parties that have come to be photographed. There's also a beekeeper, whose honey is sought after by neighbors who believe that eating local honey is an effective way of warding off allergies.

The Botanic Garden was founded as part of the Brooklyn Institute of Arts and Sciences, which also operated the museum and the Academy of Music, and there is hardly anyone in Brooklyn who doesn't call it the Botanical Garden. Its conservatory is a 1917 Kew Gardens-style greenhouse designed by McKim, Mead, & White, and along with a desert and a jungle it contains an impressive collection of bonsai trees. In fact the whole garden has a decidedly Eastern air from the Ryoanji stone and sand garden to the Japanese Hill and Pond Garden (complete with Shinto shrine, a pond in the shape of the Chinese character meaning "heart," and

ABOVE,
The Botanic Garden's cherry trees
OPPOSITE,
The Japanese Hill and Pond Garden

torii gate), which during World War II was suddenly renamed the Oriental Hill and Pond Garden.

Although during the 1960s and 1970s families and entire neighborhoods took over a number of empty lots to create small unofficial parks and vegetable gardens, the Botanic Garden was the last major inland area set aside for outdoor public use. In the twentieth century the usable open spaces of Brooklyn were found along the ocean. Olmsted himself had misgivings about oceanfront being suitable parkland for city people, for he suspected that crashing waves and roiling surf might only add to the urbanite's sense of chaos and conflict, while a still lake was by its very nature calming. But Olmsted had died in 1903, and Calvert Vaux eight years earlier, when one foggy November night he walked off a pier in Gravesend Bay, perhaps by accident, and drowned.

With the oceanfront parks Brooklyn would return to its first experiment in park building: landfill. Marine Park, Plum Beach, Canarsie Beach Park, the Floyd Bennett Field section of Gateway National Park, and even Canarsie Pol—a man-made island reserved for nesting birds—are all built, at least in part, upon the garbage and sewer sludge of a busy borough. Canarsie Beach Park is built up around the stub of a pier that was the first step of a 1914 attempt to turn Jamaica Bay into an ocean harbor that would be greater than the ports of Liverpool, Hamburg, and Rotterdam *combined* (or so said the promoters). The origins of Marine Park go back to 1911, when local philanthropists began buying up swampy waterfront land, including the site of a Revolutionary War gristmill, which they donated to the city in 1920. In the 1930s a map of Marine Park was published showing a lush landscape with boating lagoons, a riding ring, and a golf course, when in fact the golf course was 75 percent under water and the riding ring was the backyard of a police station. (In the 1940s Robert Moses, the parks commissioner, excused that earlier map as "merely a gesture.") As more city sludge was pumped in to expand the park there began what the *Eagle* called the Battle of the Big Stench, and Gerritsen Beach, site of the old mill, became commonly known as Garbage Beach. But in the end the *Eagle* and local citizens' groups won their battle to substitute sandy landfill for the sludge. Today the golf course is 100 percent above water, and although the park has been only minimally developed, kite fliers claim it is one of the best flying spots in the city.

On one side of the channel that leads to Marine Park is Dead *Plum Beach*
Horse Bay, site of the old rendering works and glue factories on
what used to be called Barren Island. With a landfill mixture of
garbage and "urban rubble" the island became a peninsula and
home of Floyd Bennett Field, New York's first commercial airport.
It is also headquarters of Gateway National Recreation Area, the
country's first urban national park, which spreads across twenty-six
thousand acres of Queens, Brooklyn, Staten Island, and Sandy Hook
(New Jersey) shoreline at the gateway to New York Harbor.
About nine thousand of those acres, on the Brooklyn–Queens border, are occupied by the Jamaica Bay Wildlife Refuge, about six
thousand acres of which are under water. The refuge, more man-
made land designed to become "wild," is the home of owls, egrets,
rare upland sandpipers, and grasshopper sparrows, and seasonal
home to migrating ducks and geese. More than a hundred pairs of
glossy ibis live there, birds that had been unknown in the New

York area for almost a hundred years before their return in 1961. The refuge is also the home of such ordinary creatures as rabbits, opossum, and a few city rats that have joined their wilder cousins. It may be the only bird sanctuary in the world that has a subway stop—on the Rockaway line—at its center.

Brooklyn now has about six thousand acres of parkland, a figure that doesn't include the cemeteries or the national park. In a very real way much of Brooklyn is a wilder, more natural place than it was a hundred years ago. Whitman wrote of "Brooklyn of ample hills" and called it the city "in a nest of water-bays," but when he wrote these lines, those newly built-up hills had been cleared of their trees and the parks were still raw with fresh plantings. As for the bays, they are only now beginning to recover from the flood of industrial pollution that began in the mid-nineteenth century. In Green-Wood's 1853 book of "hints" to plot holders it warned against planting too many trees for fear of losing the spectacular view of the harbor. It was a justified worry, for today through the groves of trees the once-dramatic sweep of the bay has been reduced to glimpses.

From the top of Lookout Hill, the highest point in Prospect Park, Olmsted claimed to see "a large sweep of ocean, the Highlands of Navesink [in northern New Jersey], Sandy Hook and all the outer harbor of New York." Today there is no view from the hilltop, just a young forest and the wrecked chassis of a car that has somehow been driven there and abandoned. Near the base of the hill is a stone monument to the Maryland troops killed in the Revolutionary War battle in August 1776. It bears as an inscription the improbable-sounding statement George Washington supposedly made during the fight: "Good God! What Brave Fellows I Must This Day Lose." Over it, with spray paint, someone has written, "Scientology Has Helped Millions of People Disolve THEIR PROBLEMS FOR GOOD!" Until a few years ago within sight of the monument stood an ancient elm that was a mature tree when Washington's men retreated past it. It fell one night of old age and rot.

Prospect Park and its clientele have changed over the years. Olmsted had intended for the grounds to be locked up at sundown. He thought it impossible for a park to be both interestingly designed and safe at night, but in New York parks are never empty.

A turning point in the way parks were used probably came in 1895, when Brooklyn judge—and later mayor of New York—William J. Gaynor ruled in several cases that boys could indeed play baseball in the parks on Sundays. Gaynor, who lived across from the Montauk Club at the edge of Prospect Park, ordered policemen to return the bats and baseballs they had confiscated, telling them, "A ball game is better for them than the temptations and allurements I need not mention to you."

A Prospect Park ranger at work

Today Prospect Park is used more intensively than Olmsted and Vaux could ever have imagined. The sterile paved area around a concrete band shell has become an unofficial center for roller hockey. Runners and bicyclists circle the park at all hours. Tai-chi classes are held on the Nethermead, where Washington's great elm once stood. Kites, illegal in New York's parks until Mayor John Lindsay's administration in the mid-1960s, fill the Long Meadow. West Indians in crisp whites play cricket at one end of the meadow, and decidedly less anglophile West Indians hold a giant carnival, with parade floats and Mardi Gras-style costumes, at the edge of the park each Labor Day.

Prospect Park, like all New York's parks, has been mistreated and cruelly used, but it has its friends. Near the boathouse on the Lullwater is a strangely contorted tree that looks something like a giant version of the bonsai in the Botanic Garden conservatory. It's the Camperdown elm, a weeping variety of Scotch elm, which was planted there in 1872. In the late 1960s it was discovered to be in danger of dying. Marianne Moore, who for years lived next to Fort Greene Park, wrote a poem about the tree that concluded:

> Props are needed and tree-food. It is still leafing;
> still there. *Mortal* though. We must save it. It is
> our crowning curio.

"The Camperdown Elm" ran in *The New Yorker*, and the tree—and perhaps Miss Moore as well—became the symbolic rallying point for those who wanted to protect the park, "still leafing. . . . *Mortal* though."

The animals Olmsted and Vaux planned for and had brought to the park—deer for the deer paddock, sheep to keep the Long Meadow trimmed, cows for the dairy—are gone. But others have taken their place. Runners complain of a pack of wild dogs that lives in the old Friends Cemetery on Quaker Hill, while on the other side of the park domestic cats (*Felis catus*) have run wild and moved into the zoo's outdoor bear pits, where they share the artificial caves with the black bears (*Ursus americanus*). Another animal is more legendary. It is the fox the Botanic Garden supposedly secretly protects to keep its grounds free of rodents. Garden officials say there is no such animal. Others say they have

seen its tracks in the Botanic Garden or across the road in Prospect Park—tracks in the snow, perhaps, crossing the park's rose garden with its round pools and then moving on down the hill to the Vale of Cashmere, where the thin, twisting pond is frozen over, and on through a pass where a concrete post once held a bronze marker decorated with a patriotic eagle commemorating a white oak that had been chopped down on an August morning in 1776.

The Camperdown Elm

CHAPTER FOUR
A City Having Fun

"They all drink here," Nicasius de Sille wrote in 1653, "from the moment they are able to lick a spoon." De Sille, an early Brooklyn settler, was Peter Stuyvesant's financial advisor and, with his *Description of the Founding or Beginning of New Utrecht*, became Brooklyn's first historian.

The De Silles had a curiously modern-sounding suburban marriage. While Nicasius journeyed to his office in New Amsterdam, Catherina stayed in their rambling stone house in New Utrecht with the youngest of the five children from his first marriage. The house, which stood for nearly two hundred years until it was torn down in 1850, was something of a showplace with its thick walls, imported red tile roof, and its own stockade to ward off Indian attacks. But Catherina had been a barmaid in her father's tavern before she married, and sleepy village life bored her. She took to secret and then not-so-secret drinking, until Nicasius asked Stuyvesant's permission to get a divorce because of his wife's "public habitual drunkenness." The governor refused, and Nicasius turned to writing melancholy religious verse, becoming Brooklyn's first poet with such lines as:

> He comforts who in pain and sorrow are;
> His power is inexpressible and grand.
> Oh God, stretch out to us Thy helping hand,
> And keep Thy children in Thy tender care.

A Calvinist God—worshipped in tiny octagon-shaped churches—
and West Indian rum were the principal diversions in early
Brooklyn, and with the De Silles the two seem to have been combined in a single household.

Unlike the New England Puritans, the New York Dutch did not
frown on religious occasions being turned into public celebrations.
Christmas was a holiday, and so were St. Valentine's Day (instead of sending cards girls went about with tiny colored whips
playfully lashing boys who caught their fancy), Easter (colored
eggs were exchanged), and *Paas*, the Monday after Easter, when
Lenten vows were forgotten and public drunkenness was perfectly
acceptable. Even slaves had a day of their own, *Pinkster dagh*
(Pentecost), on which they were free to drink as much as any
white man. Usually falling on the first Monday in June, *Pinkster*
remained an unofficial black holiday in Brooklyn until well into
the nineteenth century. Even funerals could be festive. Among the
items included on a list of expenses for an eighteenth-century funeral in Flatbush were:

> 20 gallons good wine
> 2   ”   spirits
> 1 large loaf of lump sugar
> ½ doz. nutmegs
> ½ gros long pipes
> 4 lbs. tobacco
> 1½ dozen of black silk handkerchiefs
> 6 loaves of bread

Drinking, however, was far too serious a matter to be limited to
special holidays, and taverns sprang up all across the county. Except for the country inns, most of them were along the waterfront,
where the patrons' "card playing, profanity and other vices," as a
nineteenth-century historian phrased it, "became a most serious
nuisance to the better part of the community." The nuisance was
so great the village of Brooklyn's first mayor was elected on a platform of only two planks: He was against unfenced pigs being allowed to roam the streets, and he was against the proliferation of
saloons. The Protestant churches banded together to form a Sunday school union, a public library was formed, and an academy
of music was planned, all to give the grog shops some competition.

Finally it was the Germans of Williamsburgh, with their Gothic brick breweries and their wholesome-looking outdoor beer gardens, who made everyday public drinking respectably middle-class. One brewery boasted not only a beer garden (with band concerts) but also bowling alleys, a hotel with indoor and outdoor ballrooms, a bicycle riding ring, and an ornamental fountain. By the 1890s an inn on Coney Island could claim to use up, over the course of a summer, 10,000 kegs of lager beer, or about 1,500,000 glasses—enough to support a small brewery.

Brooklyn has had its share of exotic bars, such as the Thirteen Club of Brighton Beach, in which thirteen tables were set with thirteen chairs, and thirteen waiters served an assortment of thirteen drinks while overhead the place was lighted by thirteen moons. But a more typical bar was Pat Diamond's at the corner of Ninth Street and Seventh Avenue in Park Slope, where on a summer night in 1938 an archetypical Brooklyn crime took place. Pat's son Bill was behind the bar, and the customers included Frank Krug from Albany, who was visiting in the neighborhood, and Robert Joyce, a regular. "The Dodgers," said Bill, making conversation. "Whoever first called them bums was right." Frank from Albany agreed. "It takes the Giants to show them up as bums, too," he said. "Shut up," Joyce said. "Lay off the Dodgers." Some-one—it was later thought to have been Frank—said only a jerk would be a Dodgers fan. Joyce walked out, leaving his beer on the bar, and returned in a few minutes with a pistol. "A jerk," he said, "I'll show you who's a jerk" and shot Frank through the head. He then turned on Bill, getting him in the stomach. When the police picked him up, Joyce was in tears. He hadn't meant to kill Frank or wound Bill, he said. It's just that he had taken all he could about the Dodgers.

The standard Brooklyn bar is a neighborhood place where the same crowd turns up just about every night and where even the songs on the jukebox offer few surprises. If there is any trouble, it usually involves strangers. Walt Whitman, when he wanted to mix with a literary crowd, went over to Pfaff's beer cellar on Broadway in Manhattan. Brooklyn drinkers still follow his ex-ample. For excitement they leave town, but for quiet, steady drink-ing—provided certain delicate subjects are avoided—there's a bar in every neighborhood.

Restaurants that are thought by Manhattanites to be "typically

Brooklyn" have come and gone over the years: Lundy's stucco Moorish grotto out in Sheepshead Bay, where for as far as the eye could see tables full of people downed clams and bluefish as fast as the elaborately complaining waiters could bring them; Gargiulo's, the Italian palazzo that's in—but definitely, it would have you know, not of—Coney Island; Peter Luger Steak House near the Williamsburg Bridge, as famous for its sawdust-covered floors as its massive steaks; Junior's, near Flatbush and Fulton, a brightly lit all-night hamburger place that features free pickles and architectonic ice cream sundaes and never quite got over a Manhattan magazine's claim that it had the best cheesecake in the city (the *whole* city of New York, not just Brooklyn).

The restaurant most people associate with Brooklyn is Gage & Tollner (established 1879), which makes much these days of being one of the oldest and classiest eating places in the borough. It advertises itself as "The Very Famous Restaurant in Brooklyn" (perhaps so people won't confuse it with Nathan's on Coney Island, which calls itself simply Nathan's Famous). With its mahogany tables, arched mirrors, and brass-and-cut-glass gas lights, its dining room doesn't seem to have changed since Charles M. Gage and Eugene Tollner moved their chophouse to its present location in 1889. The waiters seem to have been around almost as long, and the hash marks on their sleeves (perhaps an influence of the nearby Navy Yard) indicate their years of good and faithful service: a gold eagle, twenty-five years; a gold star, five years; a gold bar, one year.

When John McNulty, the bard and chronicler of Manhattan's Irish saloons, visited G&T in 1957, he was impressed by the popularity of whale steak and concluded that it was because whale—despite its meaty taste and mammalian origins—was classified as seafood by the Roman Catholic Church and could therefore be eaten sinlessly on Fridays. Whale steak is no longer on the menu, and pan-roast clam bellies now outsell the steaks and chops, but Gage & Tollner is probably the only place in town that still lists a "Brooklyn" on the drinks menu (a little lime, a little grenadine, and a lot of dark rum).

One of the sober institutions founded to make a stand against demon rum, the Brooklyn Academy of Music opened in 1861 and stood on the Heights until it burned down in 1903. Although there

Gage & Tollner

was some opposition to theater groups' using the academy—theater being apparently less morally uplifting than the symphony or the opera—it became a regular stop for touring acting companies. Edwin Forrest, Edwin Booth, Joseph Jefferson, Sarah Bernhardt, Laura Keene, and John Wilkes Booth all appeared there before the fire. In 1908 the academy reopened in its present grander quarters, which then included an opera house, a theater, a lecture hall, and a ballroom. Mme. Ernestine Schumann-Heink gave a preview recital in October, and a month later Caruso and Geraldine Farrar appeared in *Faust* for the grand opening. Isadora Duncan, Pavlova, Nijinsky, and Lillian Russell performed in the opera house, as did Toscanini, Paderewski, Gustav Mahler, Horowitz, and Rachmaninoff, while the lecture hall was visited by Gertrude Stein, Booker T. Washington, Helen Keller, and the admirals Perry and Byrd.

The Metropolitan Opera established a Brooklyn "season," although the *Brooklyn Daily Eagle*'s letters column was regularly filled with complaints that the Met did not offer Brooklyn its best work. The Met, on the other hand, might have suspected that Brooklyn treated its appearances there as little more than social occasions. The *Eagle*'s account of the Met's 1921 opening night at the academy began, "Quite the largest and probably the most brilliant audience of recent seasons was represented in the boxes, orchestra and balcony of the Academy of Music . . ." and went on for twenty or so inches, mentioning the names of people seen in the audience and describing the women's gowns (black jet was especially popular that year) but omitting the name of the opera itself. Two years later there was a change of fashion. The headline read "Trailing Wisps of Chiffon and Velvet Cause Male Escorts to Tread Softly," and after several paragraphs the opera, *Andrea Chénier*, was mentioned in passing.

There is a legend that Caruso died on the stage of the academy, but it is only a legend. The last time he appeared there, as Nemerino in *L'Elisir d'Amore*, he began spitting up blood during Act I, and members of the chorus passed him towels, which he coughed into and then dropped into the orchestra pit. During intermission it was announced that Caruso would continue if the audience wished. They begged him to stop—but the next night he sang a complete performance of *La Forza del Destino* at the Metropolitan Opera House in Manhattan, which probably only compounded Brooklyn's paranoia over its treatment by Met stars. The tenor died nine months later in Naples.

Over the years the academy fell on hard times. The Met no longer came to call; the house was no longer visited by major touring companies; and it soon became best known in the neighborhood for its Sunday afternoon travelogues. To help make ends meet, space was rented out for judo classes.

Then, in the 1960s, under new management and using the explosive acronym BAM, the academy came alive as it never had before. It became the New York headquarters for dance and theater companies from across the country and around the world. Local drama companies were formed, and productions were exported to Broadway. The Brooklyn Philharmonia was revitalized and changed its name to the Brooklyn Philharmonic. The old theaters were cleaned up and renovated. The old ballroom became a Performing Space. Quiche and white wine were sold in the lobby. Special buses were chartered from Times Square. People came all the way to Brooklyn—which turned out to be not so very far—to see what was happening at BAM.

Before the rebirth of the academy the most permanent sign of the theater in Brooklyn had been a stone monument in Green-Wood Cemetery in memory of the two performers and nearly three hundred members of the audience who died in the Brooklyn Theater fire of December 5, 1876. It was, the *Eagle* said, "the most awful calamity in the theater anywhere." But Brooklyn wasn't without theater. There had been the Spooner Stock Company, which performed such tried and true war-horses as *The Three Musketeers*, *Uncle Tom's Cabin* (based on the novel by Henry Ward Beecher's sister), and *The Old Homestead*. The Montauk Theater was visited by traveling companies, such as Sir Johnston Forbes-Robertson's, William Gillette's, David Warfield's, and even Sir Herbert Beerbohm Tree's. There were Yiddish theaters in Brownsville. And of course there were the downtown vaudeville and movie houses, the Fox, the Paramount, and the Albee, which went from Weber and Fields to the big bands and Frank Sinatra to disc jockey Murray the K and touring rock groups. The Fox and the Albee are gone, and the Paramount, with its forty-four hundred seats, has been rebuilt and recycled as an academic building, the eminently respectable-sounding Founders Hall of the Brooklyn branch of Long Island University.

Another of the sober alternatives to saloon life, the Brooklyn Sunday School Union, itself became something of a public spectacle with its annual parade. Henry Ward Beecher called it Saint Children's Day, "the most charming day of the year," and Walt Whitman said, "The sight of these pleasant girls and boys, marching athwart the city in every direction, was a sight to make a man's heart grow gentler." (In 1940, however, the borough president wasn't in the least inspired to gentleness when he proclaimed, "We are going to watch one hundred thousand children march for the greatest general ever known . . . Jesus Christ.")

The Sunday School Union was founded in 1816, and in 1829 some people at the Sands Street Methodist Church organized the first parade. The church has since been torn down to build the

approaches to the Brooklyn Bridge, but the tradition of the parade has continued, making it one of Brooklyn's longest-running street events. Schools are let out for the day, usually in the first week of June, and rather than being one single parade it is actually dozens of small parades that march through neighborhoods all over the borough. In recent years the holiday has been called Brooklyn Day, but in Gilbert Sorrentino's novel *Crystal Vision*, an Italian Bay Ridge boy remembers its being called Protestant Day, and his friend recalls that "Sister Augustine told us that if we even looked at the parade by accident we'd probably go blind."

To rival the Protestants' June parade, the Fourth of July parades in many neighborhoods have become Catholic festivals, with block-long "living rosaries" carried through the streets, each bead the size of a bowling ball, the crucifix bearing an almost life-sized Jesus.

But Brooklyn's oldest and most colorful Catholic street fair is

The annual Sunday School Union Parade, ca. 1910, passes through Prospect Park. (LIHS)

the annual July dancing of the eighty-five-foot-tall *giglio* outside Our Lady of Mount Carmel Shrine Church in Williamsburg. The tradition began in the late 1880s, when immigrants from Nola, near Naples, decided to honor their town's patron saint the way they did back home. According to legend Saint Paulinus, a fifth-century bishop of Nola, was carried off by Moors after he exchanged places with a hostage they were holding. A Turkish sultan, hearing of the bishop's sacrifice, arranged for a Moorish ship to return him home, where he was greeted by his townspeople waving lilies (*giglie*). As the festival has evolved in Brooklyn, the bishop's return is reenacted by the arrival of a three-ton flower-bedecked galleon (complete with crew, sultan, and attending orchestra) carried on the shoulders of 150 men of the parish. It is met by the lily, the *giglio*, a four-ton tower (also complete with an orchestra, a statue of the saint, and sometimes a monsignor or two) which looms over the roofs of the neighborhood brownstones as it is danced back and forth, carried by an additional 150 muscular parishioners. The festival builds up for several weeks, with the boat being carried some nights and the *giglio* others, until the feast day Sunday afternoon. Then both are danced, and the streets are filled with spectators and sausage and calzone vendors.

Many of Brooklyn's block parties have grown out of such religious feast days or even patriotic holidays (both American and imported), and originally most of them were truly parties for people who lived on the block. The street was roped off and tables were set out with kegs of beer and, in some neighborhoods, gallon jugs of wine. Food was prepared by the women of the block. Children who had grown up and moved away and old neighbors who had left the area would come back for a reunion. After dark there was dancing to an accordion or records or maybe even a live band. But over the years private block parties have become rare. Now they are combined money-raising events (often to buy new shade trees for the block) and neighborhood get-togethers. And since most of them are held in the late-summer, early-fall election campaign season, they are especially popular with politicians on limited budgets.

Of all of Brooklyn's block parties the one that sprawls the farthest is the Atlantic Antic, when for a September Sunday more than a mile of Atlantic Avenue, from the harbor to Flatbush

Avenue, is closed off to play host to every conceivable Brooklyn organization, from the Prospect Park Rangers to the Seventh-Day Adventist Pathfinders to the "Atlantic Avenue Marching Cheerleaders (30 Girls)" to the Gay Pride Marching Band, not to mention belly dancers from Mideastern restaurants and seemingly every potter, tie-dye T-shirt salesman, office seeker, falafel peddler, and petition carrier in the metropolitan area.

Each May the Scandinavians of Bay Ridge march to Leif Eriksson Park to crown a Miss Norway (one year even the crown prince of Sweden showed up), and the Irish hold an annual fair under the Brooklyn Bridge in June. But Labor Day, at least along Eastern Parkway as it approaches the museum and Grand Army Plaza, has become Brooklyn's largest ethnic celebration. As many as five hundred thousand West Indians take to the streets in a three-day carnival of calypso, reggae, steel-band competitions, and parades.

OPPOSITE LEFT,
Williamsburg's Feast of Our Lady of Mt. Carmel and St. Paulinus
OPPOSITE RIGHT,
Aboard the Gíglio
ABOVE LEFT,
The Moorish galleon
ABOVE RIGHT,
Balloons at a street festival

The Mighty Sparrow, the perennial star of the celebration, sings:

> Drinking they rum, beating they bottle and spoon
> Nobody could watch me and honestly say
> They don't like to be in Brooklyn on Labor Day.

With "every West Indian jumping up like mad," he sings, it's "just like carnival day in Trinidad." Meat pies, rice and peas, and curried goat are sold along the parade route—though to say the parade has a route is something of an exaggeration. The elaborate floats pass slowly down the Parkway or are sidetracked and hardly move at all as the dancing, including spectacular stilt dancing, picks up in beat. As the day progresses the parade simply becomes the crowds that flood the streets and move along from float to float, dancing and enjoying the costumes (angels, devils, the entire court of the Sun King, pirate bands, the chorus line of the Copa) that are the product of a year's work. Competition among the islands and island villages is serious, and an inventive float and costume designer are prized assets. But in spite of the music and the color and the creativity the carnival has unfortunately become better known in the press for its rum than for its dancing, and a typical day-after-Labor-Day headline reads: DRUNKEN PUNKS GO ON RAMPAGE AT B'KLYN FEAST.

The Mighty Sparrow's song continues:

> You can be from St. Claire or John John
> In New York all that done
> It's ain't have no "who is who"
> New York equalize you

At least, perhaps, for three days a year at carnival time. But Brooklyn does have one combination carnival, street fair, block party, restaurant, beer garden, and hot dog stand that runs just about all year long: Coney Island.

The Canarsee Indians called it Place Without Shadows, or so Coney Island's turn-of-the-century press agents liked to claim, and when Maxim Gorky visited in 1908, he seemed to agree. "The glare is everywhere," he wrote, "and nowhere a shadow." He preferred the place at night, seen from a distance: "Thousands of

Rufus Gorin, a West Indian costume-maker, displays some of his Labor Day head-dresses.

ruddy sparks glimmer in the darkness, limning in fine, sensitive outline on the black background of the sky shapely towers of miraculous castles, palaces and temples. . . . Fabulous beyond conceiving, ineffably beautiful, is this fiery scintillation."

In the glare of daylight, the Russian writer complained, "The visitor is stunned, his consciousness is withered by the intense gleam, his thoughts are routed from his mind, he becomes a particle in the crowd." In truth, Gorky decided, the crowds were drowning in a "marsh of glittering boredom," unaware of how dismal their lives really were.

Noel Coward, on the other hand, when asked why he walked out of a Coney Island sideshow without seeing the full array of freaks, said, "It's much, much too gay." And Freud, who stopped off briefly in August 1909 en route to Niagara Falls, the high point of his North American tour, also failed to notice the *angst* and called it *"ein grossartinger Wurstelprater"* (a splendid amusement park). But it was P. G. Wodehouse, yet another foreign visitor, who perhaps best summed up the island's appeal: "The principle at the bottom of Coney Island's success is the eminently sound one that what would be a brutal assault, if administered gratis, becomes a rollicking pleasure when charged for at the rate of fifteen cents per assault."

Coney Island may have picked up its name from the rabbits that once overran it. *Cony* is an English word for rabbit, and early Dutch settlers are said to have called the sandy island Konijn Hok, the Rabbit Hutch. Another theory accounting for the island's name suggests that a family named Conyn once lived on the beach and may have left a variation of their name behind when they moved on.

Although it is now a sandbar solidly linked to the rest of Brooklyn, Coney at one time really was an island, at a time when what's now called Coney Island Creek cut clear through to Sheepshead Bay. During the great storm of January 1, 1839, it was completely washed out to sea. But when the silt settled, Coney was back to stay, and in the 1840s a farsighted innkeeper built a clamshell causeway (with tollgate) out to the place without shadows and opened the Coney Island House. Its clientele seems to have been respectable enough, including the likes of Washington Irving, Herman Melville, Henry Clay, Daniel Webster, and John C. Calhoun.

An advertisement from the 1870s (NYHS)

Even P. T. Barnum and Jenny Lind dropped by. Other hotels followed, and before long, crowds were arriving just to spend a day at the beach. On one Fourth of July in the early 1840s, a Sunday, the toll collector counted over three hundred vehicles. When some Brooklyn townspeople heard the news, they complained that "it was a shameful breach of the Sabbath peace."

That set the pattern of Coney Island's history. For nearly a hundred and fifty years the island has been drawing crowds and making enemies of stay-at-homes who, often with good reason, have been shocked by what they fear may have been going on out there. For years standard newspaper items were both reports of new record-breaking crowds (often complete with photographs of the jam-packed beach) and notices of Sunday sermons decrying the evils of what more often than not was called Sodom by the Sea.

When Boss Tweed escaped from prison after his political empire fell apart, he hid out at a Coney Island bordello. When Carry Nation began to fall on hard times during her temperance campaign, she came to Coney, smashed up a few saloons and tobacco shops, and sold toy hatchets (each one personally inscribed by Mrs. Nation herself) to help make ends meet. After Legs Diamond was gunned down in Albany, his widow appeared at a Coney sideshow to lecture on the evils of crime. She did very well indeed and was saving up to open a gypsy tearoom when she made the mistake of saying there was more she could talk about. Two men, who left half-finished cigars behind on her kitchen table, dropped by one evening and shot her dead. When Woody Guthrie was no longer a crowd-pleasing curiosity from Oklahoma who made up a song a day, he came to Coney Island with his wife to raise a family and write a book. Years later, after a whole generation had discovered his music, Woody died in Kings County Hospital, and his ashes were scattered on the Coney Island breakwater. The island is a place that has had room for everyone.

By the end of the Civil War, when a number of small family hotels like Coney Island House had sprung up on the beach and the first rail connection to downtown Brooklyn was complete, *The New York Times* declared the island to be "one of the most convenient as well as pleasant resorts" near the city. And although James Gordon Bennett of the *New York Herald* found it "objectionable" ("sandy, clammy and fishy"), Coney Island property, most of which was owned by the town of Gravesend, became more valuable over the next fifteen years as local politicians wheeled and dealed, and real estate fortunes were made on the basis of promised favors and very real under-the-table payoffs.

The center of sin in the post–Civil War years was Norton's Point on the western tip of the island, where the walled-off community of Sea Gate now stands. There daytrippers from Manhattan would arrive by boat for "pic-nics" (often sponsored by such worthy organizations as Tammany Hall) and would promptly be greeted

The Fort Lowry Hotel in Bath Beach, as painted by M. Thursby in the 1890s. Fort Lowry and other Gravesend Bay resorts such as Hotel Hollywood, Victoria Chateau, Avoca Villa, Avon Beach Hotel, and the Idle Rest were early competitors for Coney Island's more genteel clientele. (PC)

by waiting prostitutes, three-card monte dealers, and pickpockets. The farther east you got on the island the more respectable things became until you reached Manhattan Beach and Oriental Point, where the dignified banker and railroad man Austin Corbin put up several grand hotels. He also introduced the island's first real estate slogan—"Swept by Ocean Breezes"—which he proclaimed across a huge billboard in Manhattan's Madison Square.

Among Corbin's guests were August Belmont, Leonard Jerome (Winston Churchill's grandfather), and various Lorillards, Whitneys, and Vanderbilts who came out for the summer horse racing at Sheepshead Bay. Sheepshead was the most fashionable of the three neighborhood tracks. (The other two were at Gravesend, where the Preakness was run for fifteen years, and at Brighton.) From May until October there was always racing at one or another of the tracks, and Anthony Comstock, spokesman for the Society for the Suppression of Vice, was horrified to report that between them he figured fifteen million dollars was wagered each summer. William Randolph Hearst ran for the governorship of New York in 1908 on an antibetting platform and lost to Charles Evans Hughes, who surprised everyone by promptly calling the legis-

lature into session to outlaw betting on horses. Two years later, for the first time in thirty years, Coney Island was without a race-track.

One of the island's most inventive scams involved the Brighton track and a three-hundred-foot-tall iron tower, complete with Otis elevator, that had been brought to Brighton Beach from the Phila-delphia Exposition in 1877. A sharp-eyed tout discovered that from the tower's observation deck he could see the finish line at the track and, of course, the colors of the winning jockey's silks. He worked out a system in which he signaled down to an accomplice outside the nearby Albemarle Hotel, who then rushed in to place a winning bet with the bookies in the hotel's poolroom. In those days before live broadcasts from the track, betting often went on

The Jockey Club Race Track at Sheepshead Bay, from an 1886 poster (LIHS)

long after the race was actually over. The pair made a tidy profit until a race occurred in which a winning horse was disqualified several minutes after it had crossed the line and after they had made their usual last-minute bet. This alerted the already suspicious bookies, and the next day workmen were busy building taller fences at the track.

The boss of the island in those days—and for nearly twenty-five years—was the Honorable John Y. McKane, a Gravesend town commissioner and superintendent of the local Methodist Sunday school, who set up a shack on the beach, bought himself a diamond-studded badge, and proclaimed himself chief of police. McKane got a cut of everything from bathing suit rentals to the leasing of waterfront property, and when something had to be built, McKane's construction company built it. His greatest claim to fame was that he was the man who made Benjamin Harrison President of the United States in 1888. Harrison lost the popular vote to Grover Cleveland but won in the electoral college, thanks to New

Brighton Pier in 1893. At the far left is the Elephant Hotel, and at the right is the Iron Tower that had been brought from the Philadelphia Centennial Exposition. (LIHS)

York State. Since Gravesend and Coney Island had only about fifteen hundred legitimate voters, while McKane's organization could, on occasion, register six thousand (using names from both Green-Wood and Washington cemeteries to give a realistic mixture of Christian and Jewish names), McKane believed he swung New York to the Republicans and Harrison. Indeed, in the Inaugural Parade, when McKane and one hundred members of the John Y. McKane Association, decked out with canes, gloves, Prince Albert coats, and top hats, passed the reviewing stand, the new President tipped his hat and bowed to the gentlemen from Coney Island.

Four years later it was a different story. This time McKane switched his votes to the Democrats and Cleveland, who didn't need them in his easy victory over Harrison. This time when the men of the McKane Association passed the reviewing stand on Pennsylvania Avenue, they raised their voices in a song composed for the occasion:

"Hurrah!" the John Y. McKanes
Shout in victorious glee.
"We're proud of all our campaigns
And our fair isle by the sea."

But this new President did not tip his hat or bow.

Back on the fair isle by the sea business was booming as the collection of amusements and curiosities the world would come to know as Coney Island slowly came together.

——— In 1871 Charles Feltman, the man who is believed to have invented the hot dog, arrived on Coney Island and opened a small stand on the beach. His great discovery (putting a boiled sausage in a sausage-shaped roll) was said to have been made four years earlier at the corner of East New York and Howard avenues in Brooklyn. After moving to the beach Feltman had to battle the clam as the local food of choice, and in his first year he counted only 3,684 customers. But eight years later he had expanded his shack into a full-sized restaurant and beer garden serving 80,000 patrons annually, who prob-

ably ate more than hot dogs. By 1887, a local historian proudly boasted, there were more hot dog stands on the island than houses of prostitution.

—— In 1875 the Prospect Park and Coney Island Railway reached the beach and other railways soon followed. Depending on the line you could get to Coney Island from the East River in as little as 35 minutes (faster than today's subways) or as much as an hour and twenty minutes.

—— In 1880 the first sideshow barker arrived with a company of out-of-work circus freaks.

—— In 1884 the first roller coaster, LaMarcus Thompson's Switchback Railway, made its first run.

The same year also saw the opening of the Elephant Hotel, the island's first famous landmark building. One hundred and twenty-two feet tall, made of wood sheathed in tin, and shaped like a huge Indian elephant with long curving tusks and an outsized howdah, the hotel was billed as "The Colossus of Architecture." An advertising card read: "Elephantine Colossus—cost over a quarter of a million dollars—Acme of Architectural triumphs—a whole seaside resort in this unique giant." To get to the observatory in the howdah, customers entered the hind leg marked Entrance and wound up a circular flight of stairs. The other rear leg—each was sixty feet around—was the exit, and one of the front legs was a tobacco shop. At night beacons shone out of the four-foot-tall eyes. The Elephant was indeed a functioning hotel, and until it burned down in 1896, you could spend the night in the trunk (eleven feet tall, eleven feet around), thigh, shoulder, hip, or cheek. Rooms were also available for shorter periods of time, and the saying "seeing the elephant" took on a special meaning. As one member of an old island family primly phrased it, "The Elephant stood spang in the middle of a neighborhood expressly designed for those who were up to no good, and thereabouts, too, complaisant young ladies abounded." Atlantic City might have had an older, smaller elephant building, but Coney Island found itself with the world's first—and perhaps only—tin, elephant-shaped red-light district.

The reporter Julian Ralph visited Coney Island the year the hotel burned down and noted that Surf Avenue and the side streets near the Elephant Hotel drew ten times as many people as the "better beaches" on the eastern end of the island. It was, he wrote in *Scribner's Magazine*, "the first made-to-order resort in America."

> Physically the place is a sort of Chinatown of little frame buildings set helter-skelter like a city full of houses in a panic. Aurally it is a riot of the noises of roller-coasters from two to six stories high; of test-your-grip machines; of shooting galleries and "see-if-you-can-hit-the-nigger's-head" contrivances; of those strange merry-go-rounds which seem to be manufactured exclusively in New Utrecht, L.I.; of animals designed by a baker of gingerbread; of razzle-dazzle rings that go all ways at once like a ship's compass; of a band of howling Sioux; of the yells of shouters in front of the freak museums; of rocking-boat devices that would make Neptune seasick

The Elephant Hotel photographed from the Iron Tower in 1889. Surf Avenue is the main street in the foreground. Gravesend Bay is in the distance. (LIHS)

if he rode in them; of "ring-the-cane-and-get-a-cigar" layouts; of yelling sea bathers; in short, of pandemonium.

As the Coney Island of legend was slowly taking shape some local promoters who called themselves an athletic club tried to introduce a new sport to the community. The sport was boxing, and although there had been secret or private matches on the island before 1899, a new law made public boxing matches legal so long as they were called theatrical entertainments. The Coney Island Athletic Club's theory was that if five thousand men would pay to watch an evening of illegal dog fights (another "private" island sport), a crowd of ten thousand could be drawn for a championship boxing card.

On June 9, 1899, Ruby Robert Fitzsimmons, the champ, was challenged by Jim Jeffries. It was the first heavyweight championship fight held in New York State, and when Jeffries knocked out Fitzsimmons in the eleventh round, it became the first boxing championship to change hands under a roof. And ten thousand men—no women were allowed in—paid a total of seventy thousand dollars to fill the Athletic Club's drafty wooden barn.

While Jeffries defended his crown at Coney Island a year later against former champion James J. Corbett, knocking out the ex-champ in the twenty-third round, the island fight everyone talked about for years was the November 3, 1899, Jeffries–Tom Sharkey match. It lasted a full and bloody twenty-five rounds, but what everyone remembered were the hundred giant light bulbs mounted over the ring and the movie cameras. It was the first boxing match filmed under lights, and it was actually filmed twice: once by the

Jim Jeffries versus Tom Sharkey, Coney Island Athletic Club, November 3, 1899 (Ring)

Biograph Company, which had set up its camera next to the ring, and again, secretly, by its rival, the Vitagraph Company, which had a camera hidden in the audience.

During the twenty-fifth round the Biograph camera jammed, while Vitagraph kept filming away. Less than a week later Vitagraph's pirated, complete film was being shown in vaudeville theaters in New York, Philadelphia, and Boston. There was nothing for Biograph to do but bring the boxers back to the Coney Island Athletic Club and restage the last round with a new referee wearing a derby and a false mustache, the real referee having moved on. Unfortunately, both fighters were now bald, perhaps from the heat of the lights, and Sharkey, the loser, had to be persuaded not to refight the round in earnest.

So, a fight that began with everyone pretending it wasn't a fight at all ended up being just what everyone was pretending it was, a theatrical performance. Less than a year later Governor Theodore Roosevelt repealed the law that made "theatrical" prize fights legal, and when boxing returned to New York a quarter of a century later, the Coney Island Athletic Club was long gone.

Three places made Coney Island more than just another amusement park at the end of a trolley line: Steeplechase Park, Luna Park, and Dreamland. Steeplechase, "The Funny Place," came first, in 1897, and outlasted the others, not shutting its doors for the last time until 1965. The creation of George Tilyou, who had begun his career as an island boy by selling boxes of genuine Coney Island sand at five cents each (bottles of genuine brine were a nickel more), Steeplechase featured an important innovation, a fence that surrounded the park. Once a customer wandered into Steeplechase, there was no way he was going to wander out again unless by way of the main gate. Its name came from an eight-horse, fourteen-hundred-foot elliptical racetrack that wound around the park. The horses were metal, and since the ride ran solely by gravity, the nag with the heaviest jockey usually won.

The original Steeplechase Park was a fifteen-acre open-air collection of rides ("Every One Original, Up-to-date and Snappy") designed to expose a lady's ankle, take couples through long, dark tunnels, or jostle bodies together. WILL SHE THROW HER ARMS AROUND YOUR NECK AND YELL? one advertised. WELL, I GUESS, YES! In 1907 the park was leveled in a spectacular eight-hour fire, after which Tilyou, always the showman, put up a sign, "Admission to the Burning Ruins—10 Cents." The next season saw a new twenty-five-acre glassed-in, roofed-over "Funny Place" bearing the familiar Steeplechase Funny Face trademark, a leering visage with forty-four gleaming teeth that may well have been the inspiration for the villainous Joker, "the clown prince of crime," in the old *Batman* comic books. The Tilyous had always been a church-going family, but after the roofed Steeplechase opened, rumor on the island was that they were going to church to pray for rain.

One of the most popular early attractions at Steeplechase was the Trip to the Moon. Joe Laurie, Jr., described it in *Variety*: "You got into a big winged thing that looked like a modern airplane and you felt like you were travelling up to the sky, and when you got out you met a lot of midgets dressed up like the people in the moon. The whole thing was mysterious and spooky and made your gal hold onto you." The Trip was owned by Skip Dundy and Frederic Thompson, and after a financial disagreement with Tilyou over who got the 60 and who got the 40 percent cut of the profits, the pair moved their attraction down the street to Captain Paul Boynton's Sea Lion Park.

Captain Paul was an explorer and an inventor (best known for his inflatable rubber kayak) whose park featured a shoot-the-chutes that splashed into a pool containing a few tame sea lions. Several times a day Captain Paul himself would come out in his rubber kayak and paddle around the sea lions. The park was in financial trouble, so Dundy and Thompson took over the whole place, redesigned it, positioned their Trip to the Moon at the main entrance, and in 1903 reopened as Luna Park.

Thompson was an architect, and unlike Steeplechase, Luna (which everyone in Brooklyn, of course, called Lunar) was a thoroughly planned entity. "I have built Luna Park on a definite architectural plan," Thompson wrote. "As it is a place of amusement, I have eliminated all classical conventional forms from its structure and taken a sort of free renaissance and Oriental type for my model, using spires and minarets wherever I could, in order to get the restive, joyous effect to be derived always from the graceful lines given in this style of architecture. It is marvelous what you can do in the way of arousing human emotions by the use you can make architecturally of simple lines."

Steeplechase Park's Funny Face gets a touch-up in 1951. (KHS)

At the center of Luna Park was Captain Paul's old shoot-the-chutes and lagoon, only now the sea lions were gone, and the chutes were rebuilt so that elephants could shoot down them on special cars. The park claimed to have America's largest elephant herd (Thompson's desk chair was even upholstered with elephant hide) as well as forty camels, all of which tramped through the Streets of Delhi exhibit. Thompson also liked towers, and every year he

ABOVE,
Luna Park in 1904
(LIHS)
LEFT,
*Helter Skelter at
Luna Park, 1906*
(PC)

built more. There were 1,221 towers in 1906, and a year later the number reached 1,326, all electrified. It was Luna Park that had so dazzled Gorky at night.

Four million visitors came to the park in 1904, and according to the official program this is what they saw:

THE STREETS OF DELHI

FIRE AND FLAMES

TRIP TO THE MOON

TWENTY THOUSAND

LEAGUES UNDER THE SEA

SHOOT THE CHUTES

THE SCENIC RAILWAY

THE CIRCLE SWING

WHIRL THE WHIRL

THE INFANT INCUBATORS

SEA ON LAND

THE FATAL WEDDING

THE OLD MILL

THE MINIATURE RAILWAY

AND THE LAUGHING SHOW

The Infant Incubators was probably Coney Island's oddest attraction, and also the longest running, appearing at one park or another from 1903 to 1943. It was, of all things, a display of live, premature babies presided over by a doctor, Martin Arthur Couney, who began his sideshow career in Berlin in 1896 with an exhibit called the *Kinderbrutanstalt*, the child hatchery. After touring various world's fairs and international expositions, he settled down at Coney Island with a collection of incubators far more sophisticated than those found in most hospitals. Indeed, Dr. Couney claimed his record of success with premature babies was far better than the average hospital's, and mothers of premature children in Brooklyn and throughout the New York area supposedly rushed their babies to him. His appeal to poor mothers was obvious. Where else could their children receive such care without cost? And every year there were much-publicized "reunions" of the good doctor's "graduates" to prove that his babies did grow to be healthy children and adults.

The doctor ran a serious operation. The babies were displayed by registered nurses, and the exhibit's barkers were called lecturers. Lecturers who made the mistake of adding jokes to their spiels were promptly fired. It was hardly a surprise, then, when in 1904 the doctor gathered up his babies and moved them to Dreamland, the dazzling new amusement park that was advertised as the classiest thing ever to hit Coney Island.

Dreamland was built on the ocean and included the old Iron Pier, so passengers on excursion boats from Manhattan could dock

Physical fitness at Luna Park, ca. 1935 (LIHS)

there without being tempted by any of the island's other attractions. Everything about it was designed to outdo Luna Park. If Luna had the usual assortment of food vendors, Dreamland had a popcorn concession run by Marie Dressler herself, direct from Broadway. Dreamland had the biggest ballroom in the nation. And when it came to music, Luna Park might have a tacky little jingle called "Meet Me Down at Luna, Lena," but Dreamland had a certified nationwide hit song in "Meet Me Tonight in Dreamland." Luna might have trained elephants, but Dreamland had a one-armed lion tamer who was rumored to be having an affair with Marie Dressler.

Everything was on a grand scale. In the Coasting Through Switzerland ride one of the country's first air conditioners was used to create a realistic alpine chill. The Canals of Venice were housed in what passed for an authentic reproduction of the Doge's Palace, while Pompeii fell on schedule inside a mammoth columned temple. In Fighting the Flames an entire hotel seemed to burn down hourly, and each time, the heroic fire department appeared to run over an innocent bystander as it rushed to the scene. At Dreamland's front gate, in the Hall of Creation, the first chapter

Dreamland's main entrance and the Hall of Creation, 1906 (PC)

of Genesis was recreated five times a day, and the giant statue of the bare-breasted woman outside was perfectly acceptable since she was obviously "biblical."

Everything was shining, dazzling, sparkling white, even the huge central tower, which was just like Seville's, only bigger—and better, since Seville's didn't light up at night.

The only problem with Dreamland was that it never really caught on with the public. The crowds came, but never the huge crowds that filled Luna and Steeplechase. Dreamland's owners, most of whom were politicians and not show people, complained that their creation was too classy for Coney Island, and orders went out to make the place more colorful. A lot of red paint was splashed around, but the crowds stayed away, and on the night of May 26, 1911, Dreamland burned down.

When the New York *World* received word that the park was on fire, the city editor decided to ignore it, assuming that it was just another Coney Island publicity stunt. As fires go, it sounds like a publicity stunt. It all began about 1:30 in the morning in Hell Gate, an indoor boat ride topped by a gigantic sculpture of a bat with its wings unfurled. The fire spread quickly through the park, reaching the circus area, where the one-armed lion tamer's beasts escaped and wandered terrified through the blaze. Toward dawn a lion appeared at the Creation gate, its mane on fire. It ran down Surf Avenue and into the Rocky Road to Dublin scenic railway, where it climbed to the top of a gimcrack reproduction of Blarney Castle and was shot dead with twenty-four bullets in its head.

The next day the lion, whose name turned out to be Black Prince, was skinned and put on display for ten cents a look. Lion's teeth were also for sale as souvenirs, and before long stories were being told all over South Brooklyn of wild animals performing circus tricks all by themselves in vacant lots. Usually the person telling the story hadn't seen them, but he had it on good authority from someone who had that a few of the escaped animals from Dreamland were still on the loose. The stories were told for years.

Dreamland was never rebuilt, and the New York City Aquarium now stands on its old site. Although Luna Park survived in name until 1949, Thompson had drunk himself to death in 1919, and the park was never quite the same afterward. Pigs replaced elephants on the shoot-the-chutes. Old towers fell and were not replaced. One

"The foundations are built for this," reads the penciled message on this 1904 postcard of the Steel Globe Tower. Although a number of investors put up money for this intended rival of Luna Park and Dreamland, the foundations were all that were ever built, and the Globe Tower was revealed to be one of Coney Island's more audacious frauds. (PC)

by one the buildings burned down, and eventually Luna closed and became first a parking lot and then a housing project.

Steeplechase, the least ambitious of the parks, survived into the early 1960s, outlasting the others with the simple formula of making the customers themselves the center of attention. People enjoyed watching other people ride the Steeplechase horses, watching the girls in their summer dresses walk unsuspectingly—and sometimes not so unsuspectingly—over the hidden air jets, watching couples try to maneuver their way over the Earthquake Stairway, a flight of stairs split in half so that one side would move up while the other moved down. Everyone at Steeplechase was on display.

By the early 1920s the subway, the boardwalk, and Nathan's had all come to Coney Island. But this was the Coney Island of the future. The new crowds had less money to spend. For a nickel you

could get to the island and for another nickel you could get a hot dog for lunch. Charlie Feltman, who still charged a dime for his hot dogs, found that the crowds, after some initial suspicion over the contents of Nathan Handwerker's half-price franks, were going to Nathan's. In 1954, when Feltman's finally went out of business, Nathan's sold fifty-five thousand hot dogs on a single day. The Cyclone, the island's greatest roller coaster, a five-hundred-foot-long ride that reached a peak eighty feet above the ground, cut its price from 25¢ to 15¢; the Infant Incubators—which returned to Luna Park after the Dreamland fire—would later cut its admission from a quarter to 20¢.

The average Coney Island crowd on a busy Sunday in the early 1900s was about a hundred thousand. After the arrival of the subway it was over a million. The high point of attendance is thought to have been July 3, 1947, when two and a half million people were estimated to have been on the beach. Today the numbers are well under the 1900 figure.

Some of the old attractions have survived. The Cyclone still rumbles over its wooden trestles. The Wonderwheel, the giant Ferris wheel, still turns. Nathan's is still open every day of the year, and few politicians resist the temptation of being photographed there on a hot summer weekend in an election year. New gypsy fortune-tellers have replaced the old, and there are still Dodgem cars, shooting galleries, and three-card monte dealers. A carnival-style park called Astroland has opened next to where Dreamland once stood. The most haunting reminder of the old Coney Island is itself not so very old. It's the parachute jump the Tilyous brought from the New York World's Fair in 1940 and placed next to the boardwalk. Today it stands like a ghostly sculpture, its knotted chains still blowing in the wind.

There is an old travelers' adage that people who live on islands rarely know how to swim. Although Coney Island has a beach and millions of its visitors have sat in the sand and watched the waves (and other people sitting in the sand), swimming took a long time to catch on in Brooklyn. In the early days few people even owned bathing suits. "Swimming costumes" were for rent all along the beach for twenty-five cents, and the careful shopper could find

Vestie E. Davis (1928–1978) was a part-time undertaker, newsstand dealer, and mortuary organist who lived in Bensonhurst and painted scenes of city life, including a number of paintings of Coney Island, which he remembered from his days as a side-show barker. This early painting shows a deserted beach with the boardwalk in the distance. Later, after he discovered "the more people I put in the faster they sell," he turned out a Nathan's hot dog stand with 300 customers, "all of them," he said, "eating or drinking." (PC)

rental places that even included a free bowl of clam chowder. But those with suits had to be careful, for until Mayor Fiorello La Guardia came out stoutly for bare-chested bathing—for men— almost all Coney Island arrests for indecent exposure involved males who dared appear on the beach with their chests uncovered. A local magistrate explained that he dealt out heavy sentences (as much as fifty dollars and ten days in jail, although it was usually just a weekend plus a Monday-morning lecture on decency) to protect the young from the sight of masculine nipples. "Women who frequent prizefights know in advance what they are going to

The Boardwalk

see," he argued. "The same cannot be said of innocent children who go to Coney Island for a day's outing." It wasn't until the 1940s, and World War II, that owning a bathing suit and knowing how to swim were at all common.

The Beach, 1896
(LIHS)

Brooklyn has gone through a series of sports fads. In the 1860s and 1870s it was ice skating. Two thousand skaters were counted on Prospect Park Lake on a single afternoon in 1871. Commercial skating rinks were built all over the city, with one in Greenpoint named the Monitor after the locally built warship. In the 1880s and 1890s the favorite sports were bicycling, bowling, and tennis.

Two hundred tennis courts were open in and around Prospect Park   *. . . and today*
in 1885, and there were twice that many tennis clubs waiting to use
them. Ninety years later park roads were again being closed on
weekends to accommodate a new bicycle craze, and many of the
old tennis courts were restored and covered with inflatable bubble
structures so that they could be used all year round. But as sports
came and went and came back again there was always baseball,
and for Brooklyn baseball was the Dodgers.

Over the years they were called the Trolley Dodgers, the Bride-
grooms (that was in 1890, when six players got married, and the

team went on to win the National League championship), the Superbas, the Robins, the Flock, and, of course, the Bums. Trolley Dodgers was Manhattan's nickname for everyone in Brooklyn in the 1880s, when the city had an aggressive new trolley car system, and it seemed a natural tag for the new professional ball team. Their stadium—grandly called Washington Park—was some raw wooden bleachers set up on a field between Fourth Avenue and Fifth on the flatlands below Park Slope. The first game was held in 1883, and the ticket taker and program seller was a young man named Charlie Ebbets.

Baseball had been played as an amateur sport in Brooklyn since the 1850s. There had been the Favorites and the Excelsiors, known as gentlemen's clubs, and the not-so-gentlemanly Atlantics, who were two hundred members strong, all registered Democrats. The Atlantics—whose home field was in Bedford-Stuyvesant—played well into the 1870s and were the first to defeat the country's original professional baseball team, the Cincinnati Red Stockings, who had gone unbeaten in sixty-nine games before visiting Brooklyn. Perhaps it would be more correct to call the Reds the country's first admittedly professional ball club. Boss Tweed of Manhattan had his own team, the Mutuals, all of its members on the payroll of the New York Sanitation Department (and perhaps including a few professional gamblers, as well), and it played in Williamsburgh on the grounds of William Cammeyer's ice-skating rink. Cammeyer's great innovation, his gift to New York baseball, was the admission ticket. Because his rink was fenced in, he could charge people ten cents to watch the Favorites or the Eckfords or the Mutuals, and during the Civil War he was said to have squeezed as many as ten thousand spectators onto his field.

Which was a good deal better than the Trolley Dodgers did at Washington Park. They tried moving to suburban East New York but found no new fans, and in 1898 they returned to a new larger Washington Park, a few blocks away from the old one, where they began to build a following. The club was then largely owned by a Maryland brewer who also owned the Baltimore Orioles, and when he decided the Dodgers' chances of winning were better than the Orioles', he looted the Baltimore club of its best players and sent them to Brooklyn. (Washington Park stood on almost the exact spot where the Maryland Volunteers had fought to their death during the Revolutionary War Battle of Brooklyn, but that's probably one of those historical ironies that shouldn't be overrated.) Meanwhile Charlie Ebbets, still doing odd jobs, had become club president and was secretly buying up all the Dodgers stock he could get his hands on. By the time the brewer was ready to loot Brooklyn to fortify Baltimore, Ebbets was able to buy him out, and the Dodgers at last became a locally owned institution.

The Dodgers were lucky enough to find a natural enemy very early in their history, the Giants of Manhattan. It was a mutual loathing that would continue until both teams abandoned New York for California. Brooklyn oddballs or attention seekers, it was later observed, might root for the Yankees, but no one, ever, was a Giants fan. Dodgers–Giants games always meant excitement. The eighteen-thousand-seat park would be filled to overflowing with Brooklyn fans—few Giants rooters ever dared follow their team across the river—and houses next to the park rented out roof and fire-escape space. Local bars did a brisk carry-out business in buckets of beer.

Brooklyn might not have had a star with the drawing power of the Giants' Christy Mathewson or a manager with the flair of the Giants' John J. McGraw, but the Dodgers nevertheless won the National League championship in 1899 and 1900 (before there was an American League), and they knew how to put on a show. In one game, while McGraw was arguing with an umpire, Ebbets shouted something from his private box. McGraw shouted something back. "Did you call me a bastard?" a furious Ebbets asked. "No," answered McGraw, "I called you a *miserable* bastard." That's the sort of thing—along with a Brooklyn win—the fans came out to see.

Rising attendance soon made it clear to Ebbets that Washington Park was too small, and he started buying up land in a swampy place called Pigtown, near the border of Flatbush in Crown Heights. There, on four and a half acres, he built the most modern ball park of its time, and since it was his field, he named it after himself. The newly planted grass had yet to come up in the outfield on opening day, April 9, 1913. The Dodgers lost 1–0 to the Phillies, but the star of the game was a young outfielder, Charles Dillon Stengel, called Casey after the initials of his hometown, Kansas City.

Although it was built in a filled-in swamp, Ebbets Field didn't have to wait long for the city to grow up around it. Beyond right field was Bedford Avenue, and behind left was Montgomery Street. The IRT subway stop was two and a half blocks away, the BMT a block closer. Three bus lines and a trolley passed nearby, but half the fans at a typical game walked to the field from their homes in the surrounding neighborhood. Over the years even players became neighbors. Duke Snider, Tommy Holmes, Rube Walker, and Carl Erskine all lived in Bay Ridge. Pee Wee Reese was on Hamilton Parkway, and Jackie Robinson lived in East Flatbush. Leo Durocher, Johnny Podres, Carl Furillo, Gino Cimoli, and Joe Black all lived, at least while they were Dodgers, near the team's business office in Brooklyn Heights. And Sandy Koufax, a Dodger who actually grew up in Brooklyn, graduated from Lafayette High School, and played on the Nathan's Famous sandlot team, was from Bensonhurst.

The early years at Ebbets Field saw the Dodgers under the avuncular leadership of Wilbert Robinson, a roly-poly, low-keyed sort, who, when asked by a new player for the team's batting and running signs, said, "We don't have any signs. Just get up there and hit the ball." "Uncle Robbie" took over in 1914 and left eighteen years later, having managed to pick up pennants in 1916 and 1920 with such players as Zach Wheat, Rube Marquard, Jake Daubert (a first baseman who made an astonishing nine thousand dollars a year), Chief Meyers, and Burleigh Grimes, who chewed slippery-elm bark and was a master of the spitball at a time when spitballs were perfectly legal.

In the 1920s and 1930s the Dodgers became famous for oddities: a game that stretched on to twenty-six innings and ended in a one-to-one tie when it was called because of darkness (the true oddity was that both starting pitchers played the whole game); a game that saw three Dodgers all end up on third base at the same time; a manager who would not play men whose names he couldn't spell; a star hitter who refused to bunt; and the World Series game when three Dodgers were put out by Cleveland's Bill Wambsganss in the only unassisted triple play in series history.

Because of their antics the club became known as the Daffiness Boys, a bunch that might have been fun to read about on the sports pages and talk about in bars but that wasn't drawing crowds at

Ebbets Field. Charlie Ebbets himself had died in 1925 and was buried in Green-Wood Cemetery, leaving the team in the unamused hands of the Brooklyn Trust Company. After calling back the old Dodger outfielder Casey Stengel and giving him the club to run for three years (Casey was best remembered for the time he tipped his

Ebbets Field, ca. 1914 (LIHS)

cap at home plate and a bird flew out from underneath it), the bank turned in 1938 to Leland Stanford MacPhail.

As general manager, Larry MacPhail almost single-handedly created what most people think of today as the Brooklyn Dodgers. He rebuilt and repainted the stadium, brought in electric lights for night games, installed Gladys Gooding at the organ, and broke the "gentlemen's agreement" of the New York club owners not to "give away their games for nothing" by allowing them to be broadcast over the radio. The decidedly un-Brooklyn-sounding voice of the Dodgers was a sweet-talking young southerner named Walter (Red) Barber. He even arranged the first televised baseball game, and on August 26, 1939, a newspaper headline announced: MAJOR LEAGUE BASEBALL MAKES ITS RADIO CAMERA DEBUT. The several dozen people in the New York area who had primitive television sets could have turned to W2XBS (NBC's experimental station) and watched Cincinnati beat the Dodgers at Ebbets Field. Afterward Red Barber interviewed the winning pitcher, Bucky Walters, who showed how to throw a curve ball.

The Dodgers' new popularity was celebrated by Dan Parker of the *Daily Mirror*, who wrote a poem that was later set to music and became something of a minor hit in at least one borough. It dealt with "Murgatroyd Darcy, a broad from Canarsie," who "went 'round with a fellow named Rodge" and spent much of her free time "dancing a rumba or jitterbug numbah" until the evening she declared:

> Leave us go root for the Dodgers, Rodgers,
> They're playing ball under lights.
> Leave us cut out all the juke jernts, Rodgers,
> Where we've been wasting our nights.
>
> So, leave us go root for the Dodgers, Rodgers
> Them Dodgers is my gallant knights.

MacPhail was a master showman, and one of his best attention-getting gimmicks was hiring the retired Babe Ruth as third-base coach. Crowds would turn up early to watch the Babe in a Dodgers uniform knock out a few balls during batting practice. Some people, perhaps even the Babe himself, thought he was being tried out for the manager's position, but in 1939, when MacPhail announced his new player–manager, it wasn't the former Yankee but the Dodgers' own shortstop Leo Durocher. Before Durocher left the team nine years later, he battled with MacPhail, the umpires, the league executives, the commissioner of baseball, and even the Catholic Youth Organization (which believed his marriage to a divorced actress, Laraine Day, set a bad moral example for the young people of Brooklyn). Outside of Brooklyn the Dodgers under Durocher's tutelage became the most hated team in the league as the number of on-the-field brawls, beaning duels, and spikings grew with each season. MacPhail, meanwhile, was buying up talent: a supposedly over-the-hill right fielder named Dixie Walker, who soon won the nickname "The People's Cherce" because of his unusual popularity with Dodgers fans; a nineteen-year-old called Pistol Pete Reiser, hailed by the sports writers as "the finest young ballplayer in the land" and awarded a special hundred dollar bonus; and a young shortstop named Harold (Pee Wee) Reese. Soon after Reese joined the club, Durocher became a nonplaying manager.

In 1941, with the help of Durocher's tactics and MacPhail's pocketbook, the Dodgers won the National League pennant for the first time in twenty-one years. Bunting went up on Borough Hall. A parade marched down Flatbush Avenue and Fulton Street. Fans filled the streets and didn't stop cheering, even for a long-winded speech by the borough president. Then, just as it would in 1947, 1949, 1952, 1953, 1955, and 1956, the team went off to do battle with the Yankees of the Bronx.

And after the 1941 series was over the *Eagle* ran—for the first of many times—what was to become its most famous headline: WAIT TILL NEXT YEAR. A subhead read, "Bad Breaks Cost Our Boys the Series," while the lead editorial concluded, "We can't lose the Series next year. Why, it's certain." But the following year Brooklyn was nowhere in the running.

With the outbreak of World War II Larry MacPhail left the Dodgers to join the Army. (During the First World War he had devised a scheme for kidnapping the kaiser, and perhaps he had similar plans for Hitler.) He was replaced by Branch Rickey, a quiet, professional sort, who didn't drink, didn't swear ("Judas Priest!" was said to be as profane as he got), didn't attend Sunday games, and kept a close watch over the ledger books. He was the ideal boss for a baseball team owned by a bank. John Lardner described him as "a man opposed to Sunday baseball except when the gate receipts exceeded $5,000."

Rickey spent the war years signing up any available ballplayer with even the slightest suggestion of talent and nursing along a shaky Dodgers team made up of young kids (a sixteen-year-old named Tommy Brown, a nineteen-year-old called Gil Hodges) and tired forty-year-olds like Babe Herman. In 1945 Rickey got the Dodgers off the sports pages and onto page one by announcing that he had signed a black infielder from ULCA named Jackie Robinson for the club's Montreal farm team. Two years later Robinson was playing at Ebbets Field as the first black major leaguer, and during that season when sportswriters referred to "the muscular Negro," there wasn't the slightest doubt whom they were writing about. But more blacks were on the way. A year later Roy Campanella joined the team, and a year after that it was Don Newcombe's turn.

Although all-black professional baseball teams, such as the Royal Giants and the Cuban Giants (*Cuban*, *Royal*, and *Giants*, all code words for "black," were used in sometimes confusing variations by clubs in the Negro Leagues), had played for years at Saratoga Park, Rickey called together local black ministers before Robinson's first game with the Dodgers to tell them how he expected members of their congregations to behave when Robinson took the field. "We don't want Negroes to form gala welcoming committees, to form parades to the ball park every night. We don't want Negroes to strut, to wear badges," he told them. "We don't want Negroes in the stands gambling, drunk, fighting, being arrested. We don't want Jackie wined and dined until he is fat and futile. . . ."

But he didn't say that he didn't want them to buy tickets, and on opening day, April 15, 1947, Ebbets Field was jammed with a crowd blacker and better dressed than usual. People who had never seen a professional ball game before came out in their Sunday best, wearing badges that read "I'm for Jackie." The Dodgers beat Boston 5–3. Robinson went hitless, but baseball would never be the same again.

During the next few years Durocher went off to manage the

hated Giants (thereby winning the eternal epithet "de roach" in Brooklyn); Walter O'Malley, the club lawyer, following the example of former ticket taker Charlie Ebbets, ended up one morning as the club owner; Rickey left for Pittsburgh; and new names appeared in the Dodgers' lineup: Duke Snider, Carl Furillo, Carl Erskine, Joe Black, Billy Cox, Preacher Roe, Clem Labine.

More than ever the postwar Dodgers fans themselves became part of the show. There was Hilda Chester out in the left-field bleachers, armed with a cowbell in each hand and a large sign reading "Hilda is Here." To the annoyance of visiting left fielders she rarely missed a game. Behind home plate another regular blew up balloons and shouted for his favorite, Cookie Lavagetto. And there was the Dodger Sym-phoney, eight gentlemen who had two things in common: They were all Italians from Williamsburg and they couldn't read music. They attended most evening and weekend games, sitting in Section 8 (perhaps there was some Army humor in that), seats 1 through 8. The Sym-phoney was a brass and percussion group best known for its renditions of "Three Blind Mice" (for the umpires) and "The Worms Crawl In, the Worms Crawl Out" (for opponents who struck out).

The field itself was also part of the act. It was by now the smallest stadium in the league, small enough for the fans to watch the players' faces. Part of Duke Snider's great success in the outfield was his ability to play the ball as it caromed off the field's odd angles like a master billiards player. The billboards themselves were a pop artist's dream come true. THE DODGERS USE LIFEBUOY, one proclaimed. There was a Schaefer beer sign in which the *H* would light up for hits, and an *E* for errors. The most famous of all was that for Abe Stark's clothing store on Pitkin Avenue. HIT SIGN, WIN SUIT, it read, but since it was only four feet tall and nearly four hundred feet from home plate, Stark didn't have to give away many suits. (He was, though, elected borough president, probably due as much to his sign as to the efficiency of the Democratic machine.)

Each year there was the end-of-the-season race to see if the Dodgers would be playing the Yankees in the World Series, and then came the Series itself, which, except for one year, always ended in heartbreak. Heartbreak in 1951 came in the final game of the National League playoffs at the Polo Grounds, when the Giants'

Bobby Thomson, with runners on second and third bases, the score 4–2 Dodgers, hit his famous home run, "the shot heard 'round the world" and Brooklyn went back across the river without the pennant. But in 1955 the Dodgers finally did it. For the sixth time they met the Yankees in the World Series, and this time, managed by Walter Alston, they won. WORLD CHAMPS! the headline in the *Daily Mirror* read. DODGERS DOOD IT, BUMS AIN'T BUMS—ANYMORE! BEDLAM IN B'KLYN ON 2–0 WIN. The *Daily News* ran a variation on the old *Eagle* headline with THIS IS NEXT YEAR. As for the *Eagle*, after all those years of waiting it had gone out of business in January.

The following season Marianne Moore, a Fort Greene Dodgers fan, wrote a poem entitled "Hometown Piece for Messrs. Alston and Reese." It ended:

Ebbets Field,
as seen
by Boston Globe
sports cartoonist
Gene Mack (Mack)

> You've got plenty: Jackie Robinson
> and Campy and big Newk, and Dodgerdom again
> watching everything you do. You won last year. Come on.

There was another series with the Yankees that year, but the Dodgers didn't "come on." O'Malley was already hinting about moving the team to another city, although the farewells to Brooklyn were protracted. Weekly "Keep the Dodgers" rallies were held outside Borough Hall. Local bankers and politicians proclaimed their love for the *Brooklyn* Dodgers, as opposed to possible Queens, New Jersey, or Los Angeles Dodgers, but the simple fact was that even as world champions in 1956 the team was losing money in New York. Tiny Ebbets Field, with its seventy-five-cent bleacher seats, had become dangerously rickety. The last game the Dodgers played at home was on September 24, 1957, and fewer than seven thousand people came out to watch Brooklyn beat the Pirates 3–0. The last Dodger to bat was Gil Hodges, and he struck out. When it was all over, Gladys Gooding, still playing the electric organ on the first-base line, broke into "May the Good Lord Bless and Keep You" but was interrupted by a recording of the Dodgers' theme song:

> Oh, follow the Dodgers
> Follow the Dodgers around
> The infield, the outfield
> The catcher and that fellow on the mound
>
> There's a ball club in Brooklyn
> The team they call "Dem Bums"
> But keep your eyes right on them
> And watch for hits and runs

When the recording ended, she began "Auld Lang Syne," but by then the field was covered with fans carrying off anything they could lift: patches of turf, home plate, pieces of the outfield fence.

Two facts nicely symbolize the difference between the Brooklyn and Los Angeles Dodgers. The parking lot at Ebbets Field held only seven hundred cars, while the new stadium in Chavez Ravine would accommodate twenty-four thousand. That's one. The other is that the editor of one of the Los Angeles newspapers, when he

Yankee Stadium, October 4, 1955, 3:43 P.M., the bottom of the ninth inning of the seventh game of the World Series: Elston Howard is thrown out at first by Pee Wee Reese, and Brooklyn fans storm the field to surround pitcher Johnny Podres, who shut out the Yankees 2–0. The Dodgers were World Champions. (Wide World)

heard the Dodgers' franchise was on the way, ruled that the offending phrase "Dem Bums" would never appear on his pages. Some of the fun was going out of Brooklyn, but it wasn't traveling west with the team to the land of the freeways.

With the loss of the Dodgers, Brooklyn, a community of neighborhoods almost as decentralized as Los Angeles, lost one interest the whole borough had in common. It also lost its national presence. As the years went by and people began to forget about the Brooklyn Dodgers and Dem Bums, names like Flatbush and Canarsie no longer had exotic, even magic overtones. Comedians could no longer get an easy laugh by mentioning one word: Brooklyn. The borough was in danger of becoming as ordinary a place as the Bronx, Queens, or Staten Island.

But the Dodgers, the Brooklyn Dodgers, haven't been completely forgotten. "Wait till next year" probably means more to most Americans than that other 1941 slogan, "Remember Pearl Harbor." And for all the people who have forgotten that the Bums did eventually beat the Yankees in a Series, hardly a third of October goes by without some sportswriter somewhere turning out a column about the October afternoon when Bobby Thomson hit Ralph Branca's pitch into the lower deck of the Polo Grounds' left-field stands and all of Brooklyn went into mourning.

CHAPTER FIVE
A City of Neighborhoods and People

Greenpoint, the Brooklyn peninsula that leans into the East River toward Manhattan's Twenty-third Street, was for years so isolated from the rest of Brooklyn that its residents had to pay an extra two cents a letter to get their mail delivered. Otherwise they had to troop down to the post office in Williamsburg, and getting there by foot or streetcar was often a good deal more difficult than taking a ferryboat to the Lower East Side.

Even today, on a sunny, cloudless morning, nowhere else in Brooklyn seems closer to Manhattan. The Point has never been a wealthy area; and except for its churches, a few banks, and Charles Pratt's Astral Apartments, it is a place of modest three- or four-story houses more often than not modernized by fresh aluminum siding, Perma-stone, or asbestos shingling. But overhead, just above the houses' low skyline, shining like the dream that brought thousands of Middle-Europeans to the Point's foundries, potteries, and gasworks, gleam the towers of Manhattan.

St. Stanislaus Kostka's, the largest Polish congregation in Brooklyn and perhaps in all of New York City, is there. So are the St. Elias Greek Rite Catholic Church (formerly the Greenpoint Dutch Reformed), the Church of the Annunciation (Lithuanian language Masses at 8:00 and 11:00, English at 9:30), and most dramatic of all, the Russian Orthodox Cathedral of the Trans-

figuration with its five onionshaped copper domes. Just down the   *Greenpoint*
block are the Holy Ghost Ukrainian Church ("$1,000 Bingo, Satur-
day at 7 P.M.") and the newer Iglesia Bautista Calvario (*"Bien
venidos"*).

Bedford Avenue begins in Greenpoint, follows the river until
it reaches the Williamsburg Bridge, and then cuts directly
south across the borough and through Williamsburg, Bedford-
Stuyvesant, Crown Heights, and Flatbush to Sheepshead Bay and

the ocean. To follow Bedford from one end to the other is to encounter many different Brooklyns.

Number One Bedford, a wedge-shaped building on the corner
of Manhattan Avenue (a street that oddly enough leads not toward
Manhattan but toward Queens), is the Triangle Bar, "Dancing and
Entertainment Nitely." At 10:30 on a Friday morning it supports
two bartenders (one male, one female) and a single customer
nursing a bottle of Miller. Across the street are Dombrowski &
Sons Flowershop (Est. 1906), the Katolicki Urzad Migracy J NY
(the Catholic Migration Office), and a travel agency featuring
package tours of Poland. Down the block, opposite McCarren Park,

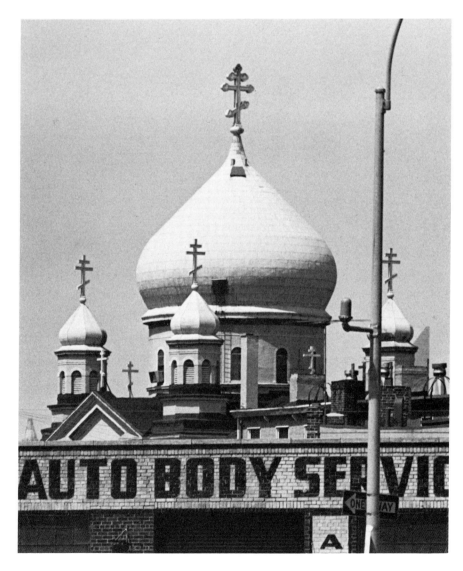

*Russian Orthodox
Cathedral of the
Transfiguration*

once the site of a foundry and tin works, is the High School of Automotive Trades. In 1937, when the school was built, the Board of Education carved over its front entrance: MANHOOD, SERVICE, LABOR, CITIZENSHIP; today, although girls are free to pass through those portals, few do. "It's still primarily a boys' school," says a teacher standing on the front steps watching the students, mostly black, file past. "Greenpoint girls are pretty traditional." He doesn't pronounce it "Greenpernt," the way cab drivers did in thirties and forties Hollywood movies.

Farther on are a newsstand that offers a choice of the *Daily News*, *Nowy Dziennik* ("The Only Polish Language Paper in New York"), and *Gwiazda Polarna* (of Stevens Point, Wisconsin, and presumably the only Polish paper published *there*), and a pet shop specializing in satisfying the needs of pigeon raisers. "I have three kinds of customers," says the proprietor, who sits out front on a folding chair. "People who grow 'em to show 'em, people who grow 'em to race 'em, and people who grow 'em to eat 'em. Most of 'em show 'em." Across the street are Belinda's Lounge ("Go-Go Girls 3:30 P.M. to 4:00 A.M.") and a storefront display that offers what may become the "new" Greenpoint. The New York Harbour Development Corporation hopes to build a thousand or so "upper middle class" riverfront co-ops connected by "glass-enclosed sky-walks." They even promise a new ferry service to Manhattan. But old-time Greenpointers are suspicious of any outfit that spells *harbor* with a *u* and worry about what those upper middle class river dwellers with their private ferryboat are going to do to a community in which the average annual income is less than fifteen thousand dollars.

In *A Tree Grows in Brooklyn*, one of those novels whose titles have added more to literature than the book itself, Betty Smith describes the area on the Greenpoint–Williamsburg border in 1912 as "serene" and then goes on to describe the tree—the ailanthus. Ailanthus trees had been imported from China to New Jersey in the 1840s in the hope that its leaves would provide a happy home for silkworms. The worms ignored it, but it proved to be especially adaptable to city life. Betty Smith wrote:

No matter where a seed fell, it made a tree that struggled to reach the sky. It grew in boarded-up lots and out

St. Stanislaus Kostka

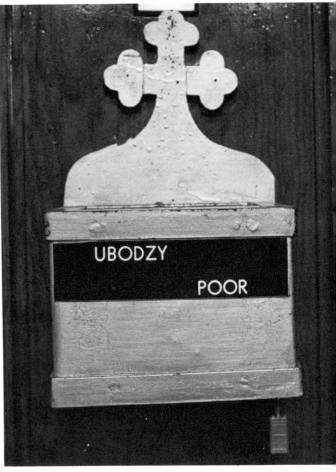

of neglected rubbish heaps and it was the only tree that grew out of cement. It grew lushly, but only in tenement districts. You took a walk on a Sunday afternoon and came to a nice neighborhood, very refined. You saw one of those trees through the iron gate leading to someone's yard and you knew that soon that section of Brooklyn would get to be a tenement district. The tree knew. It came first. . . . That was the kind of tree it was. It liked the poor.

Today a lot of ailanthus trees grow along Bedford Avenue as it approaches the Williamsburg Bridge. (Just as they do, if truth be known, in untended backyards in high-rent Brooklyn Heights. In spite of Betty Smith's lyricism the tree doesn't love the poor. It loves the city. The rich simply had gardeners to weed it out.) But

ABOVE,
The interior of St. Stanislaus Kostka

RIGHT,
A boy and his pigeons

there are also community gardens which have been carved out of abandoned lots. In one, behind a high Cyclone fence and amid a few pink flamingos, plaster Virgins, rustic benches, and some home-made signs ("Marianna's Garden: Give us this day. . . ."), carefully tended walks lead to beds of eggplants, pole beans, squash, zucchini, carrots, and even clumps of marigolds. "The soil's great here," says an urban farmer as he locks the gate, tests the chain, and puts a brown bag full of cucumbers in the back of his plumbing van. "You can grow anything here except maybe corn. We've had no luck with corn."

Just down Bedford from the gardens once stood the community fire tower. Eighty feet tall, it was manned night and day by watch-men always on the alert to sound a bell at the slightest hint of fire in Greenpoint or Williamsburg. The watch lasted until the tower itself managed to burn down in 1873, a year after the avenue suffered another brush with ignominy. With a great deal of fanfare Bedford had then become the first "modern" paved road in Brooklyn. "Modern" meant that it was paved not with brick or stone but with a new artificial wonder, a mixture of tar and gravel with the impressively nautical name of scrimshaw. Unfortunately scrimshaw, unlike the later asphalt or macadam, melted in the summer heat, and the avenue became a slippery tar pit.

As Bedford approaches the Williamsburg Bridge it passes a pretty drab stretch of real estate these days—the Iglesia Pentecostal Roca de Horeb, rows of brownstones turned into rooming houses—but in 1859 John Brown himself was carried down this street on the way from his funeral to the farm near Lake Placid where he would be buried and lie amoulderin' in his grave. John Milton Stearns, an undertaker who lived on Bedford near the corner of South Third Street, was so proud of his part in the Brown funeral, according to a local historian, that he had the body of the abolitionist martyr brought to the Stearns parlor at No. 327, where it was admired briefly by a select group of friends and neighbors.

Bedford passes under the bridge and the heaps of wrecked, rusted cars that have been abandoned there, past the "members only" storefront clubhouse of the Las Piedras baseball team, and into modern Williamsburg. Betty Smith had found the area "serene." Henry Miller, who also grew up there, found it boiling over with energy:

I remember, with a vividness as if it were etched in acid, the grim, soot-covered walls and chimneys of the tin factory opposite us and the bright, circular pieces of tin that were strewn in the street . . . I remember the iron-works where the red furnace glowed and men walked toward the glowing pit with huge shovels in their hands, while outside were the shallow wooden forms like coffins with rods through them on which you scraped your shins or broke your neck. I remember the black hands of the iron-molders, the grit that had sunk so deep into the skin that nothing could remove it, not soap, nor elbow grease, nor money, nor love, nor death.

*Eldert Street,
July 4, 1907*
(NYHS)

Miller, the son of a prosperous German-born tailor, wrote those lines from *Black Spring* in Paris, remembering, perhaps, a less middle-class Williamsburg life than he actually lived. Along Bedford Avenue today it is Betty Smith's serene city you see, the one

with trees growing out of the broken cement, and not Henry
Miller's brawling one. The grand yellow-brick and sandstone mansions still stand (one of them once a "members only" gentlemen's
club presided over by the poet William Cullen Bryant), as do the
limestone villas and terra-cotta encrusted castles of Williamsburg's old beer barons and sugar-refinery owners. But now they
have signs in Hebrew over their doors: Young Israel of Brooklyn,
Congregation Arugeth Habosem, Yeshiva Yesoda Hatora of Adas
Yereim.

At the edge of the triangular park at Division Street—which
Henry Miller remembered as having had a fountain at its center, a
place where boys would meet on Sunday mornings with their bikes
and set off for Coney Island—the Seneca Club Regular Democrats
Organization ("Abraham Gerges and Patricia Garcia Exec. Members") stands side by side with the Central Rabbinical Council of
the USA & Canada and the Talmud Torah Bnei Leivy D'Tosh, all
in nearly identical walk-up brownstones. Behind them, toward the
old Navy Yard, are blocks of low-rent high-rise apartment buildings that look no more out of place in Brooklyn than they would
in Detroit, Titograd, or Tel Aviv. Near the gash the Brooklyn-
Queens Expressway cuts through the neighborhood a boxcar-
shaped building that looks like an early roadside diner sells only
take-out kosher food.

The Jews of Williamsburg are mostly from Eastern Europe,
mostly Hasidic, mostly of the Satmar branch of Hasidism. Perhaps
as many as forty-five thousand Satmar Jews live near the Division
Street triangle, and they operate five synagogues, fifteen schools,
and an entire incorporated village in the Catskills. Hasidism is a
fairly recent movement, growing out of a spiritual revival that
swept Poland in the eighteenth century, and like most revivalist
religious groups it has splintered into many sects. The Satmars
(named for the Rumanian town of Satu Mare—"St. Mary," ironi-
cally enough—where its founders first lived) live in Williamsburg.
The Lubavitchers, considered more worldly and evangelical, have
their headquarters on Eastern Parkway, and the Belz Hasidim,
although based in Israel, have a sizable settlement near Prospect
Park. The Satmars do not recognize Israel and believe that there
can be no Jewish state until it is created by the Messiah. When the
Belz grand rabbi visited New York from Jerusalem in 1981, bal-

loons with his picture appeared along Bedford Avenue and in the diamond district in Manhattan, where many Satmar men work. The balloons were labeled "Zionist. Bust me."

Bedford Avenue, Williamsburg

Congregation Arugath Habosem: men worship on the main floor of the synagogue, women on the open balcony above them.

What unites the Hasidim (Hebrew for "the pious ones") is their belief that worship is more important than religious scholarship. Hours, even lifetimes, devoted to the study of the Talmud are not as valuable to them as direct celebration of the Creator and his works. Hasidic services are emotional, full of singing and dancing (men with men, women with women), and although their anti-quated dress and isolation have led many outsiders to compare the Hasidim with the Amish, the homegrown American sect they most

Lee Avenue, Williamsburg

resemble is the Shakers, whose ecstatic, musical, sexually segre- gated Sabbath services would probably not seem so very outlandish in Satmar Williamsburg.

Hasidic dress cannot be ignored on Bedford Avenue. The women wear high-necked dresses with long sleeves, and if they are mar- ried, they wear wigs. Small boys with their yarmulkes let their sidelocks grow into long *payess*, and as they become older they will have beards and the kind of shiny dark suits that might lead a Catholic to assume they are perpetually preparing for their first Communion. Although most men wear long, black coats and broad-brimmed fur hats called *bibers*, dress becomes more complex with higher status in the community. A most revered rabbi would have a beard, sidelocks, a *shtreimel* (a black hat trimmed in sable), a long black overcoat made of silk with pockets in the back, shoes like slippers, without laces, and white knee-socks into which he would tuck his trousers.

On Friday evening the Hasidim walk in crowds to synagogues on the side streets off Bedford. To a homeward-bound commuter stuck in a traffic jam on the Brooklyn-Queens Expressway, the silhouettes of those dark figures crossing the Bedford Avenue overpass must seem far less real than a summer stock company of *Fiddler on the Roof*.

There were, of course, Jews in Brooklyn before the Williamsburg Bridge opened in 1903, but the bridge became known as the Jews' Bridge (to the *New York Herald* it was the Jews' Highway) because it brought a new kind of Jew to Williamsburg. The traditional Brooklyn Jew had been German and middle class, the sort of gentleman who would arrive early at his office at the brewery and name the new brand of lager after the Wagnerian opera he had seen the night before. The new Jews, who came by the thousands, from Eastern Europe (or at least from farther east than Germany) via the Lower East Side of Manhattan, were described by the *Hebrew Standard* in 1894 as "miserably darkened Hebrews" with whom "the thoroughly acclimated American Jew . . . has no religious, social or intellectual ties."

In 1898, while the bridge was still under construction and the first trickle of the new Jews had begun to arrive, the *Brooklyn Daily Eagle* noted, in just about the only negative comment in its special issue in honor of the consolidation of Brooklyn and New York, that Brownsville, an out-of-the-way neighborhood tucked between Bedford-Stuyvesant and Canarsie, had "very much deteriorated by the settling there of a low class of Hebrews who have disfigured many of the dwellings by converting them into small business places." On the other hand more than one Brownsville rabbi called the area "the Jerusalem of America."

Brownsville became known as an early home of the Socialist Labor Movement, as the site of Margaret Sanger's first birth control clinic, and—to its eternal embarrassment, since such things shouldn't happen in a Jewish neighborhood—as the home of the

*Brownstones
become
synagogues*

Murder, Inc. mob. The neighborhood also inspired some notable
books: Henry Roth's *Call It Sleep* (which is to Brownsville what
Moby-Dick is to Nantucket), Irving Shulman's *The Amboy Dukes*
(before *The Blackboard Jungle* and *West Side Story* it formed
most American teenagers' impressions of what New York gang
life was supposed to be like), and Alfred Kazin's *A Walker in the
City*.

Kazin describes the neighborhood:

> We were the end of the line. We were the children of the
> immigrants who had camped at the city's back door, in
> New York's rawest, remotest, cheapest ghetto, enclosed
> on one side by the Canarsie flats and on the other by the
> hallowed middle-class districts that showed us the way to
> New York.

The curious thing about Brownsville was that it wasn't a fine
old neighborhood that had been turned into a slum. It had been

built as one. Although a post–Civil War real estate developer named Charles S. Brown had tried promoting the area as a middle-class suburb, he failed, and in 1887 a group of speculators put up tenements and began encouraging Lower East Siders to move there. Two years later the El, the elevated railway, reached Brownsville, and by 1899 Jacob Riis, the acknowledged expert on such things, officially declared the neighborhood a "nasty, little slum."

In 1925 there were over 285,000 Jews living in Brownsville and its neighbor villages East New York and New Lots, making the three the biggest Jewish settlement in the city. (The Lower East Side had a Jewish population of about 264,000 and Williamsburg 104,000.) It was, someone said, a neighborhood of Jewish tailors trying to organize a garment workers union. Emma Goldman, the anarchist, opened an ice cream parlor in Brownsville, but it went broke in three months. Norman Thomas taught adult education classes at the Labor Lyceum, and one year the New York Anarchists Club tried to hold a Yom Kippur Ball, but it was shut down by the police.

It was just the sort of neighborhood, Margaret Sanger thought, where she could open an antiabortion contraception clinic without attracting much outraged attention. She rented space at 46 Amboy Street and printed five thousand handbills in English, Yiddish, and Italian announcing the grand opening. On October 16, 1916, the doors of the first such clinic in America opened to a hundred and fifty waiting clients, and nine days later they were closed after a raid by the vice squad. The landlord evicted the clinic for "creating a public nuisance," and Margaret Sanger herself was given a thirty-day jail sentence.

As for Murder, Inc., which newspaper readers began hearing about in the early 1940s, Brownsville residents were quick to point out that although the gang used a candy store at the corner of Saratoga and Livonia avenues as a meeting place, none of its members actually seemed to *live* in Brownsville. Also, they noted, the name Murder, Inc. had been made up by a newspaperman, Henry Feeny of the *New York World Telegram*, and the gang was not really a professional killing-for-hire operation at all. Although Abe ("Kid Twist") Reles, a local hoodlum who became the state's chief witness against the gang—whatever it was properly called—claimed he and his associates had killed more than fifty people in New York, New Jersey, and the Catskills (a couple of dozen of whom had been dumped in Brownsville and East New York vacant lots), all of the deceased were working criminals who had made the mistake of trying to horn in on already spoken-for territory.

One of the victims Kid Twist apparently considered a criminal was Peter Panto, a young Italian dock worker from Red Hook who was organizing longshoremen to resist the Mob-controlled waterfront unions. Long after Panto mysteriously disappeared, Reles identified a grave on the New Jersey mud flats as being his. Before the Panto and other Murder, Inc. killings could come to trial, however, Reles managed to fall to his death from an open window on the seventeenth floor of the Half-Moon Hotel in Coney Island. He was being guarded at the time by several policemen and members of the district attorney's office.

Old Brownsvillers who claim Murder, Inc. never really existed will probably also say that Brownsville and East New York no longer exist, but they do. The El still runs there to abandoned-looking (mostly inhabited) brick tenements, a few battered newer housing developments, ailanthus-clogged lots, and a still commercially active Pitkin Avenue. It's now a black neighborhood at the very bottom of Brooklyn's economic ladder, but Brownsville, New Lots, and East New York were never neighborhoods where people lingered long.

George Gershwin was born in East New York. Isidor Isaac

RIGHT, *A Williamsburg school bus*
LOWER LEFT, *The site, in the 1940s, of Murder, Inc.'s favorite candy store*
LOWER RIGHT, *A Muslim enclave on Bushwick Avenue*

Rabi, the 1944 Nobel prize winner in physics, was from New Lots. Brownsville produced the comedians: Phil Silvers, Henny Youngman, Sam Levenson, and Jerry Lewis. Silvers once told the columnist Earl Wilson that although Lewis might have been born in Brownsville, he was quickly packed off to Newark: "We realized at an early age that Jerry didn't belong in Brooklyn." Other Brownsville boys included Al Capp, Red Holtzman, Sol Hurok, Joe Papp, and Danny Kaye, who not only became famous but also married Sylvia Fine, the daughter of the neighborhood dentist.

The Jews who settled at the Brooklyn end of the Williamsburg Bridge have not moved on so quickly. Bedford Avenue, as it turns away from the bridge and crosses over the Brooklyn-Queens Expressway, is lined with parked yellow school buses that take stu-

dents to dozens of local yeshivas and workers to their jobs in printing shops and diamond-cutting lofts in Manhattan, the buses being a more dependable way of getting home before sunset on holy days than the subway system.

A little beyond the Brooklyn-Queens Expressway the avenue begins to change. Hebrew and Yiddish signs thin out, and the old mansions are replaced with rows of four- and five-story brownstones, the front steps to the "parlor floors" having been removed so that the buildings could be divided more easily into small apartments. The rows are broken by open lots for used-truck sales, yellow-brick auto parts stores, and body shops. The Temple Beth-El turns out to be a Protestant church. There's St. John the Baptist Council 4986 of the Knights of Columbus, the Midnight Owl Van Club, the North Carolina Country-Style Store ("Featuring Southern Products from Georgia, Florida and South Carolina"), the Powerhouse Church, and Bernie's Live Farm Poultry ("You Tried All the Rest, Buy Em Live & You Buy the Best").

Bedford Avenue has entered Bedford-Stuyvesant, the second largest black community in America, second only to Chicago's South Side. There's a myth that blacks came to the white neighborhood of Bedford in 1936 when the A train, the subway made famous by Duke Ellington, took its first run from Harlem to Nostrand Avenue and Fulton Street. It wasn't really that simple.

The all-black communities of Carrville and Weeksville were established in the 1830s, and the 1841 tax roll listed families of "colored people" living there. "Not a single white person [lived] among them," a white noted, "except those who kept stores and got rich off them. . . ." At Howard's Halfway House blacks and whites could drink together, but only so long as the blacks kept to the east end of the bar. In 1855 a Colored Political Association of black property owners was formed "for the purpose of consolidating . . . political power as voters," although it wasn't until nearly a hundred years later, in 1948, that Brooklyn—and Bed-Stuy—had its first elected black official, Councilman Bertram Baker.

Brooklyn had had one of the largest slave populations north of the Mason-Dixon line, but in the nineteenth century it became a haven for the new black middle class. In 1895 *The New York Times* lamented that as soon as blacks "amass a considerable fortune they move from the city across the East River" to Brooklyn, where

Bedford, 1776 (Stiles)

living conditions were better. In the Weeksville-Carrville area, orphanages and other charitable enterprises were run by blacks rather than, as was usual, by white philanthropists and social workers who "looked after" their poorer black brothers' and sisters' needs. After the 1880s Brooklyn schools had something of a modified open enrollment policy which allowed blacks, if they wished, to attend the white schools. Most, however, chose to remain at the three segregated black schools, a choice supported by many black teachers, who feared, with some justification, that they would lose their jobs in a completely integrated system.

A great turning point occurred in 1893, when something had to be done about Weeksville's dilapidated wooden schoolhouse. Instead of being replaced, the school was merged, over the protests of many white parents, with the newly built P.S. 83 into a school of a thousand white students, two hundred blacks (a far higher percentage than that of the usual token integration), a white principal with a black assistant, and a mostly white teaching staff which included four blacks who—for the first time—taught mixed classes of blacks and whites.

The race of public school teachers is often a clue to what is happening in a community. When Henry Miller attended Eastern District High School, most of the student body, he remembered, was Jewish, and the faculty "all gentiles and all rather eccentric." A generation later Alfred Kazin noted that the faculty in his high school was Jewish but the principal was gentile. Today the forty-million-dollar school that replaced Gothic Eastern District High is 98 percent black and Hispanic, and almost half the teachers in the Brooklyn public school system are black.

At the same time that blacks were slowly moving into Bedford-Stuyvesant—mostly along Myrtle Avenue, Fulton Street, and Atlantic Avenue, the routes of the El and the Long Island Rail Road—the neighborhood was becoming known for its broad avenues of grandly proportioned brownstones. They stand today, almost as good as new, along Stuyvesant, Hancock, and Jefferson. Frank Woolworth, the five-and-dime store man, moved there from upstate Watertown. Lena Horne, who grew up in her grandparents' house on Chauncey Street, doesn't remember Bed-Stuy as a black ghetto: the Irish, as she recalls it, were the local poor folk.

But signs of racial dissension began to surface. The *Eagle* carried stories about new branches of the Ku Klux Klan. The Reverend William Blackshear, of St. Matthew's Protestant Episcopal Church, announced in his parish bulletin that since there were Episcopal churches for Negroes in the neighborhood, "this parish discourages the attendance or membership in this church of members of that race." That was 1929. Blackshear was attacked by the Council of Churches, Harry Emerson Fosdick, and Reinhold Niebuhr, but he was supported by most of the letters-to-the-editor writers in the *Eagle*, and the priest of the nearby Roman Catholic Church of the Nativity wrote in *his* parish bulletin that Blackshear "deserves applause."

The first A train arrived in 1936, and four years later there were sixty-five thousand blacks in the neighborhood, enough people to move beyond "traditionally" black Myrtle, Fulton, and Atlantic

ABOVE,
*Herkimer Street,
Bedford-Stuyvesant,
1921* (LIHS)

Surely the Lord
is in
This place

GEN. 28:16

into what had been considered white areas. The word *slum* began to be used. In fact a "Bedford-Stuyvesant Slum Clearance Project" was announced in 1939, and local real estate dealers were outraged, not because of the housing project but because of its name. Someone suggested calling it the Buffalo-Rochester Slum Clearance Project, since while both Buffalo and Rochester were names of local streets, it sounded as though the slum being cleared was far from Brooklyn. Someone else suggested "The Henry Ward Beecher Project," which had a nice historical ring to it. In the end a name— Kingsborough—was made up, and Bedford-Stuyvesant's first housing project was begun. Many would follow.

After World War II more southern blacks and Caribbean Hispanics arrived. During the 1950s the black population of Kings County rose 78 percent, while for the same period the total population dropped 4 percent—the first decline in its history. Between the 1970 and 1980 censuses the total population of the borough dropped another 14 percent, to about 2,230,000 people. About 656,000 whites left, and about 67,000 new blacks arrived in town. Blacks and Hispanics spread beyond Bedford-Stuyvesant into Williamsburg, Brownsville, East New York, Bushwick, East Flatbush, and Crown Heights, and every area that became predominantly black—or "shaded," to use the euphemism favored by banks and insurance companies—began to be considered part of Bed-Stuy. Bed-Stuy meant "black." The old white neighborhoods became jumpy. "You May Take Watts, But You'll Never Take New Lots," read a sign that went up in a New Lots store window. The Hasidic Jews of Crown Heights formed a vigilante group called the Maccabees to prowl the streets. More than ever the people of Brooklyn became conscious of the boundaries of their own neighborhoods, and the new sound of the city was the barking of guard dogs.

Bedford Avenue today is dotted with similar signboards, all the same size, all black and white, with the same style of lettering, obviously from the same sign-painting shop (like the identical style signs in West Virginia coal towns where everything in sight is owned by the same mining company): Bedford-Stuyvesant Sobering Up Station, Bedford-Stuyvesant Regional Fiscal Center, Bedford-Stuyvesant Alcohol Treatment Center. Other signs, on different streets, display other government aid programs, many of

Easter Sunday, Our Lady of Victory

them with their paint now flaking away, the funding long since used up: JOIN (Job Orientation in Neighborhoods), BLEDCO (Brooklyn Local Economic Development Corporation). There are Youth in Action, Central Brooklyn Model Cities, and most successful of all, the Bedford-Stuyvesant Restoration Corporation, which was founded in 1967, promoted by Robert Kennedy, and funded with seven million dollars of federal money, another million from the Vincent Astor Foundation, nearly as much from the Ford Foundation, and perhaps as much as thirty million more in other federal funding programs.

Bed-Stuy Restoration has restored the exteriors of thirty-seven hundred homes in a ten-block area. It has underwritten home mortgages, rehabilitated nearly thirteen hundred housing units, and converted an old dairy plant on Fulton Street into a community and job-training center complete with a skating rink and the Billie Holiday Theater. With its many programs Restoration consciously set out to become the nation's largest and most technically sophisticated community development corporation, a model for troubled cities throughout the land.

But much of Bedford-Stuyvesant, despite all the official signs to the contrary and despite an unemployment rate of over 20 percent, still does not look or feel like a slum. Perhaps it's local pride; perhaps it's the presence of so much good, solid architecture; but when you come up out of the subway at Fulton and Nostrand, there is none of the sense of having reached the end of the economic line that you get when you come down from the El into Brownsville.

One of the healthiest symbols of Bed-Stuy's sense of hope is a tree—not Betty Smith's ailanthus but a *Magnolia grandiflora*, a now-giant magnolia from North Carolina that William Lemken planted in his front yard on Lafayette Street in the 1880s and that has somehow managed to survive the northern winters and flourish. It is opposite Tomkins Park (one of Olmsted and Vaux's smaller Brooklyn creations) and catty-corner across Marcy Avenue from a new block-long community vegetable garden, also flourishing, and named for the magnolia.

Bedford Avenue crosses Fulton and passes a restaurant that looks like a neighborhood McDonald's or Burger King, only the sign out front reads "West Indian Fast Foods," and runs on to the corner of Dean Street, where a heroic statue of General Ulysses

LEFT, *Bedford-Stuyvesant renovated brownstones.* RIGHT, *Hattie Carthan, founder of the Magnolia Tree Earth Center, and the* Magnolia grandiflora

S. Grant, complete with sword and astride an especially skinny horse, seems to be marching toward a medieval castle. The castle is the old 23rd Regiment National Guard armory, and with its keep, towers, crenelations, lancet windows, and even a portcullis gate, it must have been a delight to Brooklyn's nineteenth-century medievalists. The neighborhood actually has an unusual number of such fortresses. There's a castle on Jefferson and another on Marcy (on the site of Cammeyer's skating rink, one of Brooklyn's first baseball fields and later home of a National Guard unit whose awe-inspiring Civil War nickname was "The Red Legged Devils"), and still another armory stands just across Eastern Parkway. No matter what Bed-Stuy's other problems may be, it seems ideally outfitted for medieval warfare.

The statue of Grant, which, if not about to take the armory, is at least advancing on Manhattan, was a gift to the city from the Union League Club, whose clubhouse still stands across the street.

Its double-story bay windows are supported by a giant eagle with outstretched wings. Two lions, which seem to be studiously avoiding each other's gaze, hold up shields on the tile roof, and terracotta plaques of Lincoln and Grant himself are placed so they can admire the general's statue. The club no longer exists, and the building is used for offices.

Twenty-Third Regiment Armory, New York National Guard

Farther along the block are a zebra-painted nightclub, the African Islamic Mission, the Haitian-American Day Care Center, and the New Muse, a children's branch of the Brooklyn Museum, all of which seem very much in business. Walls along the street are covered with posters for the Reverend James Cleveland's concert tour and *La Nouvelle Haiti Tribune*, Brooklyn's only bilingual Haitian newspaper. Ahead is Eastern Parkway, the Eglise Baptiste Eben-Ezer, and a kosher pizza parlor.

Eastern Parkway, Olmsted and Vaux's grand tree-lined boulevard, runs along the crest of a ridge. To get to the other side, and Crown Heights, one must first cross a one-way street, then a strip of trees, then the six-lane parkway itself, another strip of trees, and finally another one-way street running in the other direction. During the Depression years and even into the early 1940s women would gather each morning among the trees in what they called the slave market. People looking for maids, waitresses, and other household help would cruise by, look over the prospects, and make job offers. The going wage was from 20¢ to 35¢ an hour.

In those days the outfield curve of Ebbets Field could be seen down Bedford Avenue as it led off toward Flatbush. Anyone these days asking for Ebbets Field will still be sent down to the corner of Montgomery and Bedford in Crown Heights, where a twenty-three-story, thirteen-hundred-unit apartment building now stands. Its official name is the Jackie Robinson Apartments at Ebbets Field, but everyone in the neighborhood calls it Ebbets, as though the stadium were still there. Next door, on the side of what used to be a shopping center, is a huge mural called *The Wall of Fame*. It shows masses of dark-skinned people marching past the pyramids of Giza and the Sphinx, crossing the river Nile, and heading toward Bedford Avenue. Some wear African dress, some are workers from Southern cotton fields, some are students or modern workers, and some wear brightly decorated Caribbean shirts and carry calypso drums. The colorful scene is bordered with portraits of historic figures, entertainers, and sports heroes, including Martin Luther King, Jr., Harriet Tubman, Malcolm X, Che Guevara, Marcus Garvey, Sojourner Truth, Toussaint L'Ouverture, and Haile Selassie; Bob Marley, Jimi Hendrix, Mahalia Jackson, Billie Holiday, and John Coltrane; and Jesse Owens, Pelé, Althea Gibson, Earl the Pearl Monroe, and Joe Louis.

Only two people pictured in the mural, which was painted during the summer of 1981 as a community project, would probably

EBBETS FIELD

recognize the neighborhood, Jackie Robinson and former congresswoman Shirley Chisholm. Shirley Chisholm was born in Brooklyn, raised there and in Barbados, and used to be fond of saying that her greatest handicap as a politician was not that she was black but that she was a woman. In 1964 she was elected to the state assembly, making her New York's first black female legislator. Washington was obviously the next step, but Bedford-Stuyvesant was then gerrymandered so that it fell into five different districts, each with a white majority, thereby effectively fragmenting the black vote.

*Jackie Robinson
Apartments
at Ebbets Field*

Gerrymandering was hardly new to Brooklyn politics. When John Y. McKane was political boss of Coney Island, for instance, he had worked out an imaginative variation on the old redistricting ploy. The court had ruled that voters must vote within their precincts rather than going to Gravesend Town Hall, where it was McKane's habit to loiter on Election Day and perhaps wield a bit of influence at the ballot box. McKane promptly redrew the districts into six pie-shaped areas with Gravesend Town Hall at the center, cut six doorways into the hall, and continued to sit next to the ballot boxes.

But Shirley Chisholm and others fought for the redistricting of Bedford-Stuyvesant through the courts and won decisions to have the lines redrawn. In 1967 she was elected to Congress, where until 1982 she represented a district that includes parts of Bedford-Stuyvesant, Crown Heights (not, incidentally, the part that contains *The Wall of Fame*), and Williamsburg.

Beyond Empire Boulevard, where the Dodgers' victory celebrations and wakes once began, Bedford Avenue enters the long stretch of middle-class residential Brooklyn that leads from the flatlands below Crown Heights to Flatbush Avenue and on to Sheepshead Bay. In the blocks before Flatbush massive squares of 1920s and 1930s apartment buildings with names like Bedford Arms, Bedford Close, Bedford Gardens, or more adventurously, The Conrad, The Lincoln, or The Van Wyck are broken up by tree-shaded side streets lined with small individual houses. Each street is guarded with an identical sign: THE BLOCK IS PATROLLED AND BLOCK WATCHED. Recent surveys seem to show that neighborhood teams of block watchers who patrol the streets in the evening don't actually cut the crime rate, but they do create a sense of neighborliness and goodwill among the block watchers. Some block associations also hire professional protection companies that patrol the streets by car. There are no grand houses in this neighborhood, which has traditionally been the first step up out of grimmer neighborhoods, and as such the houses are especially well looked after and the gardens especially neat. It is now a largely black area, as American blacks and West Indians follow the same route as the earlier immigrants, and the real estate is as lovingly tended as ever.

When Bedford reaches Church Avenue, it reaches the center of

ABOVE,
*East 17th Street,
Flatbush*

*President Street,
Crown Heights*

commercial Flatbush. "Flatbush, where," as P. G. Wodehouse wrote in a lyric for a 1917 Jerome Kern song, "there's room to swing a cat." It passes the back gate of Erasmus Hall High School, alma mater, as everyone in the neighborhood will tell you, of Barbra Streisand and Bobby Fischer, the chess champion. A Gothic stone "new" building surrounds the old wooden Erasmus Hall, which was built in 1787 to be, as someone on *The New York Times* once wrote, "the Eton of Long Island." Next door is a huge boarded-up movie palace ("For Rent"), and on a side street is Flatbush's Graustarkian town hall, also boarded up, which a community association is trying to save.

Flatbush
Reformed Church
LEFT
and parsonage
RIGHT

After Bedford crosses Flatbush, it enters a small-town USA world (about 90 percent white) that includes every style of home-town American architecture from the days of Rip Van Winkle to those of Andy Hardy to those of the Brady Bunch. Elizabethan Tudor mixes with Brentwood Moorish, often on the same block, sometimes in the same house. There are mansions pillared to rival Tara on blocks off Bedford, a wooden Japanese fantasy home, and houses crowned, for no apparent reason, with Russian onion domes or Arabic minarets. Old Dutch farmhouses (some of them authentic) alternate with classic 1910 shingle-and-stucco craftsman-style villas and glass-brick and terrazzo palazzos (with above-ground swimming pools in their backyards). For all the blandness the name Flatbush might suggest to the outside world, it contains some of the most eccentric architecture east of the Hollywood Hills.

Albemarle Road, Flatbush

Ocean Avenue, Flatbush

It even has its own "colonial Williamsburgh" on the campus of Brooklyn College, the academic home of generations of Brooklynites (ranging from Oscar Handlin to Alfred Drake to Bernie Cornfeld to Sam Levenson to Eugene Genovese to Irwin Shaw, who described it as "a wonderful school. . . . It was free and it taught me all I needed to get out of Brooklyn"). Next door to the college on Bedford Avenue is Midwood High, whose most famous graduate is Woody Allen. In 1956, as a seventeen-year-old Midwood junior, he was writing jokes and trying to sell them to New York columnists. Earl Wilson printed one of the first: "A hangover is when you don't want to come out of your room because you think your head won't fit through the door." The comedian Steve Allen, who didn't graduate from Midwood, called that line worthy of "one of Kaufman and Hart's best Broadway comedies," which may

Brooklyn College

be stretching things a bit, but it was a better start than that of
Weber and Fields, who didn't graduate from Midwood either but
who broke into the comedy business as eleven-year-olds doing their
routines on Coney Island for two dollars a day (plus five free
beers).

Beyond the college the houses along Bedford become more uniform, many of them what real estate agents call "mothers and
daughters": neat brick or stone homes with a garage in the basement and an apartment large enough for a live-in mother, or a
mother-in-law, who is always assumed to be a widow. Bedford
ends at Sheepshead Bay, the old racetrack and fishing town. The
last house is number 4817, a small white frame home with a large

spruce tree in the front yard. Next door, facing the bay and the tied-up fishing fleet, is a Sizzler Steak House.

In its nine and a half miles Bedford Avenue has gone from Ukrainian Greenpoint to Hasidic Williamsburg, Puerto Rican Williamsburg, black Bedford-Stuyvesant, "mixed" Crown Heights (including a corner of the Haitian neighborhood some call La Saline after a Port-au-Prince slum), white Flatbush, whiter Midwood, and Sheepshead Bay, with its mixture of Irish and Italians and a few black families, descendants of grooms and stableboys who arrived before the turn of the century to work at the Jockey Club racetrack.

In Brooklyn the neighborhood is everything. Clifton Fadiman, who attended Boys' High in Bed-Stuy at the same time as Irving Thalberg, recalls that Flatbush boys and Williamsburg boys both acted tough, but that Flatbush boys were just acting. Williamsburg boys were the real thing. It was an important difference to understand.

Jewish kids who lived on the Boro Park end of Prospect Park in the 1940s and 1950s were warned by their parents not to wander into Irish Park Slope and to stay clear of the Norwegian "squareheads" in Sunset Park and Bay Ridge. The Irish kids of the Slope ventured into Italian South Brooklyn only when they were looking for trouble. Time has blurred the neighborhood lines and who stands on either side, but life goes on pretty much the same. Most summers, usually when August gets hottest, there are newspaper stories about teenage "gang wars" on Fifth Avenue near Union Street, at just about the spot where the Irish used to mix it up with the Italians. Italians are still on their side of the line, but the "enemy" now speaks Spanish.

Between Sheepshead Bay, where Bedford Avenue comes to an end, and Coney Island is Brighton Beach, with its tightly packed gray apartment houses, its streets darkened by the noisy shadow of the El, and its sunny boardwalk along the ocean. Signs in store windows that read ZDYES GAVARYAT PA-RUSSKI ("Russian Spoken Here") aren't really needed, because everyone is speaking Russian anyway. There are so many Russians in Brighton Beach that they've started calling the place Little Odessa. Brooklyn has had a Russian population for years. At the turn of the century there were more Russians (24,400) in the borough than blacks (18,367). Since

The present Our Lady of Perpetual Help, the largest Roman Catholic church in Brooklyn, was dedicated in 1929. When the first Mass was celebrated at the church's original building on the same site in Sunset Park in 1894, the headline in the Brooklyn Daily Eagle *read, "Redemptorist Fathers Build a Church on the Edge of Fields."*

1972, when the Soviet Union liberalized its Jewish emigration policy, more than 30,000 Russian Jews have arrived in New York, and about 20,000 of them headed for Brighton Beach, where there are now dozens of new Russian social clubs, bars, grocery stores, and restaurants. In one of them, where all the waitresses wear crucifixes, even pork *polmeni* is on the menu. On the boardwalk the Gastronom Moscow sits almost next door to the Gastronom Odessa, which seems to be the more assimilationist of the two, since it advertises, in English, "Franks, Knishes, Heros." A few doors away is the Puerto Nuevo, which ignores all Baltic influences and offers chorizos and *alcapurrias*.

Another restaurant that's not particularly Russian—this one standing under the El—is Jack and Joe's Eat in Good Health. Brooklyn seems to have a weakness for combining food and statements of moral uplift. Park Slope has a restaurant called Purity. There's also an Economy. A Scandinavian deli on Flatbush Avenue, now torn down, had a sign over its counter reading "What You Eat Today Walks and Talks Tomorrow." A sign next to an Arabic restaurant off Atlantic Avenue proclaims "It Pays To Eat Well" (although some old-timers in the neighborhood claim the place used to be a barbershop, and the sign then read "It Pays To Look Well"). In rebellion against all this good advice is an eating place on Fifth Avenue that operates under a marquee that says GET EVEN! EAT YOUR HEART OUT.

A more isolated neighborhood is Canarsie, east of Sheepshead on Jamaica Bay. If comedians could get a laugh in Manhattan simply by saying "Brooklyn," they could bring down the house in Brooklyn by saying "Canarsie." In one standard vaudeville sketch

A Brighton Beach side street

Little Nell saves her widowed mother from the villainous banker   *Canarsie*
by paying off the mortgage with three thousand dollars she earned
in Canarsie. "Little Nell," her suspicious mother asks, "have you
been good?" "To get three thousand dollars in Canarsie," Nell answers, "you *have* to be good."

Anne Jackson, the actress, lived briefly in Canarsie when her
family moved to Brooklyn from western Pennsylvania during the
Depression. They lived directly on the Jamaica Bay mud flats in
one of a number of former summer cottages linked together by
rickety boardwalks. The *Eagle*'s description of the area was rather
romantic: "The individual with disdain for the comforts of civilization and an eye for the picturesque can still get himself a house
overlooking the melancholy reaches of Jamaica Bay for approximately $7.00 a month." The seven dollars appealed to her father;
the fireflies and seabirds appealed to Anne; but the mosquitoes
and the smell of raw sewage appealed to no one, and after the
house was almost washed out to sea during a hurricane, Mrs.
Jackson insisted that they move to higher, if more expensive,
ground in East New York.

The Jacksons wouldn't recognize Canarsie today. The mud flats have been covered with landfill, and a building boom that began in the 1950s has filled the open fields with modest one- and two-family houses, most of them occupied by their owners. There are also a few massive apartment projects, and across Fresh Creek Basin is a forty-six-building complex called Starrett City, a sort of Emerald City that dominates the horizon. Underground, just beyond Starrett, is the pride of the Brooklyn sewer system, a place referred to by one sewage enthusiast as "the Colosseum of sewers." There, a half dozen or so brick-lined channels carrying streams of sewage from eastern Brooklyn, all bubbling as cheerfully as mountain brooks, join together and move off toward a nearby sewage treatment plant. The junction is cleaner than most subway stations, and as long as the sewage flows at a rate of more than two and a half feet a second, there's no smell. According to legend alligators lurk in New York's sewers, but there isn't a creature in sight. "I hate to ruin a good story," a city official has explained, "but there just isn't much to eat in a sewer. There isn't enough to keep a rat alive, much less an eight-foot alligator."

Farther west, between Coney Island and the Verrazano-Narrows Bridge, lies Bensonhurst, which before the 1890s was simply the old Benson farm. It is a solid, quiet neighborhood—or mixture of Jewish and Italian neighborhoods that sprang up around the old Dutch Reformed Church in New Utrecht—and it has changed less *Starrett City*

than most. Although Sandy Koufax left the area with the Dodgers to live in Los Angeles, Bensonhurst has a reputation for keeping its young people, and rather than moving off to Long Island, Westchester, or New Jersey, they tend to stay close by. Belying the popular notion that the age of Italian immigration is over, Bensonhurst also attracts the immigrants of the 1980s, young couples in their twenties or early thirties who are neither tired nor weary and who arrive at *these* teeming shores with enough money for a down payment on a house.

81st Street, Bensonhurst

In the 1890s Bensonhurst-by-the-Sea had attempted to rival *18th Avenue,*
Coney Island by catering to a more middle-class clientele. An ad- *Bensonhurst*
vertising brochure promised that unlike other Atlantic coast resorts, at Bensonhurst-by-the-Sea, "No fierce gales from the east
can incommode its inhabitants, no booming surf will disturb their
slumbers, nor the sight of shipwrecks wound their feelings."
Bensonhurst-by-the-Sea and nearby Bath Beach have been buried
by landfill and the Shore Parkway, but inland Bensonhurst houses
built since the 1920s remain, often remodeled, rebuilt, enlarged,

covered with new siding. Backyard fig trees planted by grand-
fathers when they were young homeowners still bear fruit for their
grandchildren.

In Thomas Wolfe's "Only the Dead Know Brooklyn" (another
Brooklyn tale more famous for its title than for its story), a tall
stranger in a subway station—probably Wolfe himself—is a figure
of suspicion simply for wanting to get to Bensonhurst. The narrator, speaking in Wolfe's North Carolinian idea of what a Brooklyn accent sounds like, says:

> "Where yuh goin' out in Bensonhoist?" I says. "What
> numbeh are yuh lookin' for?" I says. *You* know—I
> t'ought if he told me duh address I might be able to help
> him out.
>
> "Oh," he says, "I'm not lookin' for no one. I don't know
> no one out deh."
>
> "Then whatcha goin' out deh for?" I says.
>
> "Oh," duh guy says, "I'm goin' out to see duh place,"
> he says. "I like duh sound of duh name—Bensonhoist,
> y'know—so I t'ought I'd go out an' have a look at it."
>
> "Whatcha tryin' t'hand me?" I says. "Whatcha tryin'
> to'do—kid me?" *You* know I t'ought duh guy was bein'
> wise wit me.
>
> "No," he says, "I'm tellin' yuh duh troot. I like to go
> out an' take a look at places wit nice names like dat. I
> like to go out an' look at all kinds of places," he says.
>
> "How'd yuh know deh was such a place," I says, "if
> yuh never been deh befoeh?"
>
> "Oh," he says, "I got a map."
>
> "A *map*," I says.
>
> "Sure," he says, "I got a map dat tells me about all
> dese places. I take it wit me every time I come out heah,"
> he says.
>
> And Jesus! Wit dat, he pulls it out of his pocket, an'
> so help me, but he's *got* it—he's tellin' duh troot—a big
> map of duh whole f—— place with all duh different pahts
> mahked out. You know—Canarsie an' East Noo Yawk
> an' Flatbush, Bensonhoist, Sout' Brooklyn, duh Heights,
> Bay Ridge, Greenpernt—duh whole goddam layout, he's
> got it right deh on duh map.

*Under the
fig tree in a
Bensonhurst
backyard*

"You been to any of dose places?" I says.

"Sure" he says. "I been to most of 'em. I was down in Red Hook just last night," he says.

"Jesus! Red Hook!" I says. . . .

Bocce

Red Hook—now there's an Italian waterfront neighborhood people know about, because it fits, or perhaps once did, all the popular stereotypes. Al Capone once lived on President Street, back when he was bartending at the genteelly named Harvard Inn at Coney Island. More recently Joey Gallo's mob—which Jimmy Breslin called "the gang that couldn't shoot straight"—had its headquarters in a brownstone in Red Hook, complete with Joey's dwarf associate and a lion—reportedly used to intimidate rivals and enemies—locked in the basement. Joey became something of the darling of the New York literary and show business set, their favorite house gangster, before he was gunned down early one morning in 1972 at a Manhattan restaurant.

Across Buttermilk Channel from Governors Island, Red Hook is where people were said to disappear and later wash up under the piers. A neighborhood restaurant that used to be on President Street was popular with both locals and slummers. The front room was plainly furnished with a barbershop-style black and white marble floor, wire ice-cream-parlor chairs, and Formica-topped tables. Then came the kitchen, and beyond it was a dark dining room that looked as though it were a low-budget Hollywood idea of a gangland restaurant, including heavy red drapes and gold plaster sconces. The food was good; the servings were large; and the prices were low. If the slummers were lucky, elegantly dressed couples would arrive in expensive cars and walk through the kitchen to the back dining room. The regulars ignored them. The slummers would exchange knowing looks. Just down the block from the restaurant, an old woman might be seen sitting at a front window in a widow's black dress. Locals might nod to her. Knowing slummers would claim she was "Mama," the most influential woman in Red Hook, perhaps in all of South Brooklyn.

One of the rare times Bensonhurst made news was when the jeweled crown of the madonna at the Regina Pacis Shrine Church there was stolen and returned anonymously by the thieves, who were influenced in their decision to give up the relic—some said—by Mama's boys or—others said—by some of their professional rivals. In any case, as South Brooklyn popular religious events go, the return of the crown was almost the equivalent of the ten o'clock Mass on May 17, 1953, at St. Francis Xavier's in Park Slope, when the congregation offered special prayers that many of the Dodger faithful believe broke Gil Hodges's seventy-five-game batting slump.

While Bensonhurst, with its street vendors, Italian bakeries, Jewish delis, and family-centered social life, has survived, Red Hook, cut off from the rest of Brooklyn by the Belt Parkway and the entrance to the Brooklyn-Battery Tunnel, has been dying. Although a few of its nineteenth-century row houses have been restored, most of its residential buildings have been ripped down for public housing and for new container shipping piers. The Italians have moved on and been replaced by black and Puerto Rican families that move out as soon as they can find more habitable places. The view of the Statue of Liberty from Red Hook is spectacular, but it has ceased to be a working neighborhood.

Between Bensonhurst and Red Hook used to be an area called Yellow Hook, but in 1850, when the city was swept with yellow fever and the very word *yellow* seemed a cause for panic, the name was changed to Bay Ridge. The new name, thought up by a florist, was decided upon at a meeting of the community's leading citizens, who were not unaware of what panic could do to real estate values. The community had also been called Fort Hamilton, after the mili-

19th-century warehouses, Red Hook

Coffey Street,
Red Hook

tary installation that still stands there, and the village seemed to
pride itself on a long tradition of military courtliness.

Robert E. Lee had been stationed at the fort in the early 1840s
and had made himself quite popular in the community. He planted
a tree which still grows at St. John's Episcopal Church, where he
was a vestryman, and when his friend and fellow officer Thomas
Jackson (he wouldn't become "Stonewall" until the First Battle
of Bull Run) was baptized, Lee stood up as Jackson's sponsor at

St. John's. During the Civil War, when Lee's nephew was brought to the fort as a prisoner and then locked up with other Confederate soldiers in Fort Lafayette (now under the foundation of the Brooklyn tower of the Verrazano-Narrows Bridge), the young man was much sought after by local hostesses with fond memories of his uncle. The War Department, however, was more hardhearted about such things and kept him under lock and key.

After the war Bay Ridge real estate was bought up by newly

Fort Hamilton, Bay Ridge

*Bay Ridge
Engine Company
No. 1, ca. 1890
(LIHS)*

rich industrial barons, whose architectural visions were far grander than the narrow confines of Brooklyn Heights could contain. The bluff above the Narrows was lined with castles and plantation houses, and even Diamond Jim Brady bought Lillian Russell a villa with a view of the bay. The most interesting house of the lot must have been the one built by the owner of a Williamsburg iron foundry and constructed along the same principles as the cast-iron loft buildings that were then going up in Manhattan. Contemporary comments make much of the fact that although the structure was built almost completely of copper, you would never know it to look at it. It was also fireproof, but it wasn't demolition-proof, and like all the rest of the mansions—except Lil Russell's place, which is now a private school—it has been torn down.

Today most people associate Bay Ridge and adjoining Sunset Park with Scandinavians, especially with Norwegians, although in

Lillian Russell's villa, now a private school

fact families with Italian names are in the majority. Some Italians claim that Leif Eriksson Park was really supposed to have been named after Mother Cabrini, but Parks Department officials say there is no truth to that. The park, with its rough stone monument and runic-looking lettering, is the most tangible sign of the Scandinavian presence in Brooklyn, although the bakeries and specialty shops along Fifth and Eighth avenues may be more satisfying.

Brooklyn's first Norwegian, a ship's carpenter named Hans Hansen, arrived in 1663. He promptly changed his name to Bergen, after his old hometown, and settled near the Gowanus, where there was steady work repairing ships. For over two hundred years Brooklyn's Norwegians stayed near the Gowanus and Erie Basin, until in the 1870s they began to move to rural Bay Ridge. By the time the subway arrived, in 1916, the Ridge was an old Norwegian neighborhood. The first Norwegian newspaper, the *Nordiske Blade*,

began publishing in 1878, and thirteen years later it had a competitor, the *Nordiske Tidende*. Both are still in business. Finnish and Swedish papers also began to be published in the neighborhood, the Finns having settled next to Sunset Park, which they called *Pukin Mäki*, the Goat Hill. Their neighbors were chiefly Polish gardeners who worked at nearby Green-Wood Cemetery.

The great innovation the Finns brought to America was the co-op apartment house, which was really quite common back home. The first in Brooklyn and probably in all of New York was built in 1916 at 816 Forty-third Street, the Alku I ("Beginning I"). Next door went Alku Toinen and so on until there were twenty or so scattered around Goat Hill. They also built a meeting hall, the Imatra (named after a waterfall in Finland), which is still in use as a community center and an aid society for Finnish immigrants. Every year, on a Sunday late in February, Brooklyn's Finns

Good Friday procession at Holy Cross Greek Orthodox Church

gather at the Imatra to sing, dance, and recite sections of the national epic poem, *The Kalevala*. Since Longfellow based the meter of *The Song of Hiawatha* on the rhythms of the Finnish epic, an inattentive English-speaking visitor might sit through the whole performance wondering why a bunch of Finns was carrying on so about the shores of Gitche Gummee and the shining Big-Sea-Water and the wigwam of Nokomis, daughter of the moon, Nokomis.

Until recently the greatest disaster to hit Bay Ridge took place in 1848, when a group of bored teenagers burned down the Grace Methodist Church. But in 1959, in spite of the efforts of the Save Bay Ridge Committee, feverish petition-signing campaigns, and even the burning in effigy of Robert Moses—head of the Triborough Bridge and Tunnel Authority—bulldozers arrived and began knocking down houses and rearranging the landscape in preparation for the building of Moses's great dream, a bridge—the world's longest suspension bridge—across the Narrows.

The Staten Island Chamber of Commerce wanted to call it the Staten Island Bridge—after all, Brooklyn, Manhattan, Queens, and even Williamsburg had bridges named for them—but it was eventually named, at least in part, after the Italian explorer Giovanni da Verrazano, in the hope of placating Bay Ridge's Italians. Instead it simply inspired non-Italians in the neighborhood to call it the "Guinea Gangplank."

As the bridge and its curving approach ramps were built local streets were rerouted or buried beneath tons of concrete. The project was blamed for an 8 percent drop in population, although other studies were produced to show that most of the people evicted by the construction actually stayed in the neighborhood. In time some Bay Ridgers even came to love the bridge.

Although construction began with the drilling of a hole in the foundations of Fort Lafayette, the official ground-breaking ceremony was held on friendly Staten Island, where no one had to learn to love the bridge. Real estate values there were skyrocketing. A lot that was worth twelve hundred dollars in 1958 sold for six thousand a year later. As the bridge went up speculators were busy filling the formerly wild and unsettled acres of the island with tract houses and subdivisions garnished with suitably lyrical, rural-sounding names that tried to suggest that nothing at all had changed.

Sunset Park

*A wedding party
under the
Verrazano-
Narrows Bridge*

Staten Island's rapid development repeated, less than a century later, what had happened in Brooklyn after its bridge opened. At that time speculators rushed to fill the empty spaces in neighborhoods bordering on the comfortably settled Heights and Fort Greene areas, places in South Brooklyn now called Cobble Hill, Carroll Gardens, Boerum Hill, and on to Park Slope.

Houses could be as much as twenty-five feet wide, but most developers in Park Slope and other neighborhoods found that they could buy undeveloped plots that had been planned for four twenty-five-foot houses and instead build five twenty-footers. Not only could they get the profit of an extra house that way, but with a smaller house—and in a brownstone five feet makes a considerable difference—they could appeal to a more numerous, less wealthy clientele.

Where, on the usually hundred-foot-deep lots, the houses were built was also subject to variation. Most often the front steps from the parlor floor came down to the edge of the sidewalk, leaving the houses with no front yards to speak of but giving them large, private backyards. In some areas—sections of Third Street in the Slope and many blocks in Carroll Gardens—the rows of houses were built at the back of the lots, which all but eliminated the backyards but opened up the fronts to more sunlight and made streets of ordinary width seem as broad as boulevards.

Prospective buyers were given a variety of choices within the standard row-house pattern. The houses ranged from three to five stories. Some had flat brownstone fronts; some had bay windows. There were also brick "Queen Anne" models with or without non-functional slate cupolas on the roof (the model without the cupola usually came with a small wrought-iron fence running along the front edge of the roof). From catalogues customers could choose variations on the interior design: a ten-foot-tall built-in pier glass for the parlor or a gas-lit fireplace, plain or decorated stained-glass "lights" above the front windows, an all-mahogany or a mahogany-and-tile fireplace for the back parlor (which sometimes served as the dining room), sliding doors between the parlors with etched-glass or all-wood panels, or perhaps no sliding doors at all but an archway decorated with a lattice of fancy lathe work.

The Heights, of course, has always been the grande dame of brownstone Brooklyn. It was a suburb built for lawyers, stock-brokers, and shipping magnates who made their fortunes in lower

Three Bay Ridge dwellings: Traditional, High Rise, and Eccentric

*First Place
Carroll Gardens,
1896* (LIHS)

Manhattan. Even at the end of the nineteenth century, when *Harper's Magazine* reported that the Heights wasn't what it had been "of yore" and that the new money was moving toward Bedford or out to Bay Ridge, the neighborhood kept its dignified old families in their dignified antebellum homes, whose only hints of frivolity appeared in the luxurious curves of the wrought-iron bannisters on the front steps. If, as the old saying goes, most people in Brooklyn know only the sections of town that lie between their neighborhoods and Manhattan, the people who live on the Heights need know nothing at all about Brooklyn. "Here," reported Truman Capote, a onetime Heights resident, "scarcely anyone can give directions; nobody knows where anything is, even the oldest taxi driver seems uncertain."

The people of old Brooklyn Heights didn't have to know Brooklyn, because deep in their hearts, they knew the town was theirs. To them, and to their friends across the river, Brooklyn *was* the Heights, and for nearly half a century the Heights was Henry Ward Beecher.

Like most people associated with the Heights, Beecher wasn't born there. He was "called"—as they say in the Protestant ministry—from Indianapolis in 1847 to take over the pulpit of Plymouth

Church. One of the first things he did was remove the pulpit and replace it with a platform. Mark Twain described him in action: "He went marching up and down the stage, sawing his arms in the air, howling sarcasms this way and that, discharging rockets of poetry, and exploding mines of eloquence, halting now and then to stamp his foot three times in succession to emphasize a point." To a visiting senator from Indiana, he was "a landscape painter of Christianity." Local street children were less awed. "There goes Beecher, he is a screecher," a group of boys once called after him, according to a story Beecher himself told.

When Lincoln came to Brooklyn, it wasn't to campaign for the presidency but to hear Beecher. When Charles Dickens visited, it was to lecture at the new Plymouth Church built especially for Beecher. The church was the biggest hall in town, and for one night Dickens accomplished what Beecher did every Sunday—filled all three thousand seats. After a speaking tour of England to rally support for the Northern cause during the Civil War, Beecher became famous enough to be a clue in a Sherlock Holmes story. (The fact that Watson had an unframed portrait of the preacher led Holmes to draw certain conclusions in "The Resident Patient.")

Beecher's tactic—a tactic later used with equal success by Norman Vincent Peale in Manhattan and Robert Schuller in Southern California—was not to preach hell-fire and brimstone but to stress what he called "the positive in Christianity." And he kept ahead—

LEFT,
*Willow Street,
Brooklyn Heights*
RIGHT,
*Henry Ward
Beecher's
Plymouth Church*

but not too far ahead—of popular political taste. He was not a feminist, but he was president of the American Woman Suffrage Association. He was not an abolitionist, but he preached against the institution of slavery. When he heard that Jews were being barred from resort hotels, he preached against anti-Semitism.

Beecher also had a feeling for practical comforts. His name appeared in magazine endorsements for watches, trusses, and soap. His home on Columbia Heights overlooking the harbor was described as "hung with velvet drapes and scattered with embroidered cushions, silken scarves and stuffed hummingbirds." And he wanted his parishioners to be comfortable, too. "Ye are gods," he would tell them. It was, to one critic, the "Gospel of Gush," but when Thoreau heard Beecher, he thought he detected signs of "paganism," a compliment.

Beecher's extraordinary popularity was threatened in 1874, when he was accused by an associate, Theodore Tilton, of having seduced Tilton's wife. The newspaper that broke the story sold 100,000 copies, and the adultery trial, which lasted almost six months, was the biggest national news story since the Civil War. When Beecher was not found guilty—a judgment many outside the Plymouth congregation doubted—the church raised $100,000 to pay his legal fees, and Beecher continued being Brooklyn's most famous and perhaps most respected citizen.

In this Borough of Churches the Heights skyline, even more than that of most neighborhoods, is broken by Gothic spires and finials of what used to be the society churches of Brooklyn. Designed by architects such as Richard Upjohn and James Renwick and decorated by the Tiffany family, a few are still used by their original congregations; some (such as the Church of the Pilgrims) have changed hands (now Our Lady of Lebanon); and others stand empty or are used by private schools as auditoriums. A number of less traditional religions have also found homes on the Heights. The most visible is the Jehovah's Witnesses, who have spread their dormitories along Columbia Heights, sometimes by tearing down classic old brownstones, sometimes by using the old buildings as false fronts for more modern structures hidden behind them. Witnesses move, always en masse it seems, between their dorms and their printing plants near the Brooklyn Bridge, and it is not uncommon to overhear theological discussions in which scrubbed, short-haired disciples quote back issues of *The Watchtower* to each

Library of the Long Island Historical Society, Brooklyn Heights, built in 1878

other with all the zeal and precision of Talmudic scholars.

A more obscure and far more revolutionary sect once also used the Heights for its publishing operation. At 43 Willow Place, in what is now the last row of colonnaded houses in the Heights, the Utopian Oneida Community published its newspaper, *The Circular*. At the community's headquarters in upstate New York the society was often threatened by its outraged neighbors because of what was popularly—and incorrectly—considered its policy of free love, but life in Brooklyn was peaceable. As religious tracts go, *The Circular* showed a noticeably greater sense of humor than *The Watchtower*. One of its running bits of whimsy was classified ads placed by the firm of Meek & Lowly:

> WANTED—Any amount of SHARES OF SECOND-COMING STOCK, bearing the date A.D. 70, or thereabouts. . . . ROOMS TO LET in the "Many Mansions" that Christ has prepared for those who love him.

Beecher, the Oneida Community, and presidential succession all came together in Brooklyn when a disgruntled former Oneida communard named Charles Guiteau rented an apartment in the Heights, believing he could get a job as an editor on Beecher's church newspaper. While in town he also hired a lawyer named John Dean to sue Oneida for the nine thousand dollars he claimed they owed him for the six years he had spent in the community. Beecher wouldn't hire him; Oneida wouldn't pay; but Guiteau won recognition in his own way, years later, by assassinating President James A. Garfield.

As the Heights became less noticeably fashionable in the early twentieth century it began to attract writers and artists who appreciated the quiet neighborhood, the spectacular view of the harbor, and the low rents. New residents included Hart Crane, Walker Evans, John Dos Passos, and Thomas Wolfe, who moved so often that "Wolfe Slept Here" signs could be scattered through the Heights the way "Washington Slept Here" signs cover Virginia. Wolfe came from North Carolina, via Harvard and Manhattan, to 40 Verandah Place, a narrow—and now picturesque—alley in Cobble Hill (an apartment he described in *You Can't Go Home Again* as a place "more like a dungeon than a room that a man would voluntarily elect to live in"), and then moved to two different apartments on Columbia Heights and finally to a place on Montague Terrace. Jack Kerouac claimed once to have passed Wolfe on the Brooklyn Bridge during a raging blizzard. Kerouac was fourteen at the time, visiting his Brooklyn grandmother. They passed without speaking.

Arthur Miller, who was born in Manhattan, moved to the Heights, as did Norman Rosten, who was from Coney Island; Alfred Kazin, from Brownsville; Truman Capote, from New Orleans and all points south; and Norman Mailer, who was born in New Jersey but grew up in Brooklyn and graduated from Boys' High back in the days when the smart boys were said to go there and the social ones to Erasmus. Rosten and Mailer still live on the Heights, Rosten several years ago having been named Brooklyn's Poet Laureate by the borough president, while Mailer has one of the fine old houses on Columbia Heights with a view of the city and the bridge.

Probably the most famous, or at least most singular, collection of Heights artists lived at 7 Middagh Street (now lost under the Brooklyn-Queens Expressway), where George Davis, a *Harper's Bazaar* editor, gathered together a household consisting of Carson McCullers, W. H. Auden, Paul and Jane Bowles, and—when they

*Verandah Place,
one of
Thomas Wolfe's
Brooklyn homes*

The official name on city maps is the Esplanade, but everyone calls it the Promenade, and it offers every out-of-towner's dream view of what Manhattan is supposed to look like.

were passing through town—Benjamin Britten, Christopher Isherwood, Gypsy Rose Lee, Salvador Dali, Anaïs Nin, and just about anyone else the household took a fancy to. Richard Wright and his wife and baby lived there briefly but decided it was "not a proper environment in which to raise a child" and moved back to Fort Greene, where he had written *Native Son*. McCullers and Jane Bowles, since they were the only women in the place, were soon doing all the cooking, until Gypsy Rose Lee found an out-of-work chorus girl from the Cotton Club to take over the chores.

David Smith, who became one of the century's greatest sculptors, moved to State Street in the early 1930s. As red-light districts went, State Street didn't have the flair of Sands Street on the other side of the Heights. Sands Street got the boisterous sailors whose ships were tied up at the Navy Yard, while State Street catered more to commercial seamen, whose ships docked at the foot of Atlantic Avenue. It was a less violent crowd, but State remained for years one of those streets that children raised in the Heights were told to avoid. (Atlantic Avenue, which ran parallel to State a block away, had yet to become Brooklyn's commercial Arab district. That wouldn't happen for a decade, when construction in lower Manhattan would force the Syrian and Lebanese stores to relocate.) In his diary, Smith records how he had begun to experiment with welded sculpture but unfortunately kept setting his apartment on fire. One day, while walking along Atlantic, he spotted "a long rambly junky looking shack" called the Terminal Iron Works next to the ferry dock. The next day he went in and asked if he could work there. Blackburn, who ran the place, said he didn't mind, and Smith moved in his welding equipment.

"Between Terminal Iron Works at 1 Atlantic Ave. and George Kiernan's Saloon at 13 Atlantic Ave.," Smith wrote, "I met about everyone on the waterfront." Kiernan's, another casualty of the expressway, was a "men only" saloon where, Smith wrote, "We ate lunch, got our mail. . . . It was the social hall for blocks around. Any [welding] method or technique I needed I could learn . . . from one of the habitues, and often got donated material besides. These were depression days." When Smith couldn't pay his rent to Black-

Atlantic Avenue, 1910 (LIHS)

burn, he went out to the ships with the Iron Works welders and did repair work. What he learned at Atlantic Avenue helped him create some of the most innovative and influential sculpture of his age, and when he opened his studio at Bolton Landing on Lake George, he called it the Terminal Iron Works.

Edmund Wilson had described the Heights as a burnt-out place in 1925:

The pleasant red and pink houses still worthily represent the generation of Henry Ward Beecher; but an eternal Sunday is on them now; they seem sunk in a final silence. In the streets one may catch a glimpse of a solitary well-dressed gentleman moving slowly a long way off; but in general the respectable have disappeared and only the vulgar survive.

Twenty years later, in his novel *Memoirs of Hecate County,* Wilson took another look at another part of Brooklyn and found things considerably livelier. His narrator takes a subway ride to Kings Highway, near Coney Island:

I walked along under low-columned cloisters, pale brown and a little more gracious than anything connected to the subway on the Manhattan side of the bridge; and emerged from the subway steps into the sunlight of a whole new world, which seemed to me inexplicably attractive. . . . There was space and ocean air and light, and what seemed to me—it was what most astonished me—an atmosphere of freedom and leisure quite unknown on the other side.

Hecate County was banned in New York State, for its supposed obscenity, but the *Eagle* (ignoring the fact that the book also describes Brooklyn as "miserable" and "dreary") took time out amid the controversy to run a story whose headline read:

BANNED BOOK PRAISES BORO

Brooklyn may be proud of its native sons, but nothing pleases it more than the compliments of strangers such as Wilson. William Makepeace Thackeray captivated the town by calling it "a pretty, tranquil place entirely different from New York." Talleyrand visited Brooklyn, and so did Tom Paine and Lafayette (who lifted up the young Walt Whitman in his arms, or so claimed the old Walt Whitman) and—according to legend—the young Ho Chi Minh, who supposedly worked there as a cook. F. Scott and Zelda Fitzgerald and the café set of the 1920s would come across the

Fort Greene

river to dance in the roof gardens at the Bossert and St. George hotels, the Bossert—done up like a yacht—being the more fashionable. The St. George, however, the largest hotel in the city, could boast of an Olympic-size salt water swimming pool in a mirrored Art Deco setting.

Another perhaps less welcome visitor to the Heights had for a

The St. George Hotel pool, once advertised as "the most luxurious in the world." (PC)

few years in the late 1950s a painter's studio on Fulton Street just down the block from the Puerto Rican bodega where Walt Whitman printed the first edition of *Leaves of Grass.* The building he lived in was full of studios: David Levine, the painter and caricaturist, worked there, as did the painter Burt Silverman, and Norman Mailer rented office space. The visitor, though, was especially interested in photography and shortwave radios until one day the FBI picked him up and announced that he was Colonel Rudolf Ivanovich Abel, the most important Russian spy it had ever grabbed. The building, as well as the bodega and the whole block, has since been replaced by the Cadman Plaza apartment complex.

A few years ago the borough president's office published a list of famous Brooklynites that managed to include such brief visitors as John Steinbeck, Isaac Bashevis Singer, and W. C. Fields. Among the genuine articles, however, were Aaron Copland, Eubie Blake, S. J. Perelman, Mary Tyler Moore, Beverly Sills, Eli Wallach, Lauren Bacall, Susan Hayward, Robert Merrill, Mel Brooks, Isaac Asimov, and the truest daughter of all, Mae West, whose father, Jack, was a policeman who walked the Coney Island beat. She made her debut at Coney as a third-grade dropout who tap-danced and belted out a dialect number called "My Mariooch-Maka-Da-Hoocha-Ma-Coocha," and when she died in 1981, she came home to Cypress Hills to be buried. Someone figured that during World War II Brooklyn contributed more men to the armed forces than thirty-eight states put together, which probably explains why WW II movies always included one wise guy from Flatbush wish-

ing he knew how the Dodgers were doing. Someone else figured that one out of every eight Americans is related to someone who once lived in Brooklyn, and for years the borough made much of the fact that if it were still an independent city, it would be the fourth largest in the country.

But by the beginning of the 1960s people began to worry about Brooklyn. The Dodgers were gone; Coney Island was decaying; the Navy Yard was endangered; the old neighborhoods seemed to be coming apart at their seams. A billboard went up next to the Long Island Rail Road Station on Flatbush saying:

Let's Keep the

OK

In Brooklyn!

At about the same time a new group of people began to, as they put it, "discover" Brooklyn. Manhattanites on a budget, new people in the city, even people from run-down sections of Brooklyn began to discover that the borough, perhaps the last great Victorian city in the country, was jammed with good, solid, handsome-looking houses that could be bought for what across the river was considered "almost nothing."

The Brownstone Movement, as it came to be called, began in the Heights and spread to the surrounding brownstone districts. When sections of Cobble Hill were slated for clearance for high-rise apartments, COBBLE HILL IS NOT A SLUM notices appeared overnight, stenciled on every crosswalk, and a successful campaign was waged to save the neighborhood where Winston Churchill's mother was born from being destroyed. When a church across Verandah Place from Thomas Wolfe's old apartment was torn down to be replaced by a supermarket, the neighbors saved the vacant lot and turned it into a neighborhood park.

The early Brownstoners liked to call themselves pioneers, and the people whose neighborhoods they "settled" into and "saved" were often puzzled by their zeal. Couples who had worked a lifetime to educate their children and get them out of the neighborhood found newcomers of their children's generation moving in and turning old rooming houses back into one- and two-family homes. A man named O'Hanlon, in his seventies and a lifelong Park Slope resident, told *The New York Times* that he didn't think the Brownstoners saved the neighborhood from anything but cheap rent. "I'm always amused when people call themselves pioneers," he said. "It's like the rest of us were Indians."

But the Brownstoners were indeed saving houses, blocks, and whole neighborhoods from literally falling apart. Often by doing the work themselves and by renting out a floor or two, they found a way of being able to afford a comfortable house in the city. But there were schisms. People who renovated—or even modernized—their brownstones found themselves pitted against those who believed in restoring them to their full Victorian—or more often Edwardian—glory. Entire cocktail parties could be spent debating the proper way of stripping paint from mahogany newel-posts. But it was a serious business. The Brownstoners were pouring not only their life's savings but also their life's blood into those buildings and a pioneer mystique did indeed emerge. A favorite story—it popped up in enough neighborhoods to become an almost traditional urban folktale—had to do with the Brownstoner who

ABOVE,
President Street,
Park Slope

Trompe-l'oeil
on Prospect Place
in Park Slope

ABOVE LEFT,
Cumberland Street,
Fort Greene
ABOVE RIGHT,
Seventh Avenue,
Park Slope

was about to be mugged and robbed when one of the muggers suddenly stopped and said, "Don't touch him; he lives here." That, to a true pioneer, was acceptance.

By the time the movement reached deep into South Brooklyn, Fort Greene, and out to Greenpoint, the original brownstone neighborhoods had advanced far beyond their pioneer status. The Heights, its raffish days—despite a few resistant pockets—over, was back in the hands of the stockbrokers and lawyers it was originally built for. Buildings in Carroll Gardens on the edge of Red Hook were going co-op. The old Ex-Lax factory on Atlantic Avenue became a condominium. The "Indians" of O'Hanlon's generation in Park Slope were an endangered species. Brownstoning was now often in the hands of professional speculators, but a corner had been turned. Brooklyn, if you picked the right neighborhood, was no longer a joke. In real estate circles at least, it had become "a viable alternative."

Under the veneer of the new, gentrified Brooklyn, the old Brooklyn lives on. The Brooklyn Museum may have lost its grand front staircase to modernization, but it gained two heroic Daniel Chester French statues of matrons personifying Brooklyn and Manhattan that adorned the Manhattan Bridge before *it* was modernized. Like medieval churches that treasured relics of saints, Brooklyn churches preserve bits of lost Brooklyn. The bells from the tower of the orignal Steeplechase Park, the one that burned in 1909, now chime in the steeple of Our Lady of Solace on Coney Island. Girders from the demolished Myrtle Avenue El were used in the altar of the Church of St. Michael and St. Edward in Fort Greene. And the Brooklyn accent survives. Not the Hollywood version, which never existed, or the one Manhattan sportswriters made up for colorful quotes from the fans of "Dem Bums" (Joey Adams once said that if the pitcher Waite Hoyt were injured and the headline read "Hoyt Hurt," a Brooklyn fan would pronounce it "Hurt Hoyt"), but the curiously dainty muddling of vowels that Edmund Wilson once described as "an accent worn down on the lips of the crowd as the long Brooklyn pavements had been by their feet." Children of the brownstone "pioneers" often surprised their parents by becoming oddly bilingual. At home they could speak in the accents their parents had learned in Albany or Palo Alto. On the street they could speak with the accents of Union Street and Prospect Park.

But in Brooklyn everything remains a matter of neighborhoods. At the corner of Sixth Avenue and Lincoln Place in Park Slope is a public school, and across from the school is an arched streetlight on which hang dozens of discarded sneakers and gym shoes. Down the block is a place the local kids call the sneaker factory, although it isn't a factory at all, but a discount shoe store. After they buy new sneakers, the kids tie the old ones together by the laces and throw them over the lamppost. From this corner on some days you can look down the slope and out across Buttermilk Channel to Governors Island and beyond to the hills of New Jersey. Within a few blocks of the corner are a Haitian Methodist church, an abandoned Presbyterian church, a Baptist church, an Episcopal church that seems to have been misplaced from the Cotswolds, and two Catholic churches, both of which hold Spanish-language masses, one called St. *Au*gustine by the Protestants and St. A*gus*tin by the Catholics.

The Dodgers played some of their earliest games a few blocks away in a park that now holds the empty ruin of a stone house the Parks Department put together during the Depression, supposedly out of stone from the original old house on the Gowanus around which the Revolutionary War Battle of Brooklyn raged. A few blocks in the other direction stands the Pillar of Fire Church, which narrowly missed being destroyed in December 1960, when a United Airlines DC-8 and a TWA Constellation collided over the Narrows and the DC-8 fell on Park Slope. The mansion of a nineteenth-

century opera singer is right across the street from where the plane crashed. The mansion of the inventor of Vaseline is a block away. The convent of the nuns who make the Communion wafers for the Brooklyn diocese is nearby. (Catholic girls in the neighborhood used to be warned by their parents that if they were not good, they would be sent there and put to work.) A large and mysterious building rumored to be a house of prostitution run by the black mafia is also nearby. In another house lives an old woman said to be a princess. There are at least three private or parochial schools near the corner. Gentrification has moved down the blocks toward the corner from Prospect Park. The price of houses has doubled, tripled, quadrupled. Many of the restored brownstones have gas lights out front, left over from the late 1960s, when the utility company had a special offer for new brownstone owners. Most of the children who go to the public school live in houses that don't have gas lights out front.

Standing on the corner at midnight on New Year's Eve, you can hear ships in the harbor blowing their whistles and fireworks exploding all over South Brooklyn. On other nights, when the breeze is from the harbor, as it almost always is in Park Slope, not quite buried in the blare of TV sets and the roar of cars as they race the lights up Sixth Avenue is the faint sound of sneakers slapping together like muted wind chimes.

Union Street runs down from Carroll Gardens, across the Gowanus Canal and up again to Park Slope and Grand Army Plaza.

IRVING T BUSH
1869 - 1948

ABBREVIATIONS

Gleason: *Gleason's Pictorial* newspaper
KHS: Kingsboro Historical Society
LIHS: Long Island Historical Society
LC: Library of Congress
Mack: From *Hall of Fame Cartoons, Major League Ball
 Parks*
NYHS: New-York Historical Society
PC: Private collection
Ring: *Ring* magazine
Sands: From *Old Sands Street Church*
Stiles: From *The Civil, Political, Professional and
 Ecclesiastical History and Commercial and Industrial
 Record of the County of Kings and the City of
 Brooklyn, New York*
Wide World: Wide World Photos
All uncredited photographs are by Jim Kalett

BIBLIOGRAPHY

The following is a selected bibliography of books and articles I consulted while writing *Brooklyn . . . and How It Got That Way*. I have not included sources identified in the text or such invaluable newspapers and periodicals as *The New York Times*, *The Brooklyn Daily Eagle*, *The Village Voice*, *New York*, *The Brooklyn Phoenix*, *The Prospect Press*, *The Canarsie Courier*, *The Newtown Register*, and *Harper's* (*Weekly*, *Monthly*, and *Magazine*). *JLIH* refers to the *Journal of Long Island History* published by the Long Island Historical Society, *NYHSQ* to the *New-York Historical Society Quarterly*.

Allen, Steve, *Funny People*, New York, 1982.

Anderson, Will, *The Breweries of Brooklyn*, Croton Falls, New York, 1976.

Armbruster, Eugene L., *Brooklyn's Eastern District*, Brooklyn, 1942.

Barlow, Elizabeth, *The Forests and Wetlands of New York City*, Boston, 1971.

Bliven, Bruce, Jr., *New York*, New York, 1981.

Brown, Joshua and David Ment, *Factories, Foundries and Refineries*, Brooklyn, 1980.

Bunker, John G., *Harbor & Haven*, Woodland Hills, California, 1979.

Capote, Truman, *The Dogs Bark*, New York, 1973.

Caro, Robert A., *The Power Broker*, New York, 1974.

Christman, Henry M., ed., *Walt Whitman's New York*, New York, 1963.

Connolly, Harold X., *A Ghetto Grows in Brooklyn*, New York, 1977.

Cory, David M., "Brooklyn and the Civil War," *JLIH*, 1962.

Dann, J. C., ed., *The Revolution Remembered*, Chicago, 1980.

Donovan, James B., *Strangers on a Bridge*, New York, 1964.

Edmiston, Susan, and Linda D. Cirine, *Literary New York*, Boston, 1976.

Fein, Albert, ed., *Landscape Into Cityscape*, Ithaca, New York, 1968.

Frommer, Arthur, *New York City Baseball*, New York, 1980.

Goddard, Donald, *All Fall Down*, New York, 1981.

Graham, Frank, *The Brooklyn Dodgers*, New York, 1945.

Griswold, Stephen, *Sixty Years With Plymouth Church*, New York, 1907.

Halpern, Joseph W., *Flatbush in the American Revolution*, Brooklyn, 1976.

Harding, Virginia Felter, *Memorable Green Point*, Brooklyn, 1944.

Hoffman, Jerome F. X., *The Bay Ridge Chronicles*, Brooklyn, 1976.

Honig, Donald, *The Brooklyn Dodgers*, New York, 1981.

Hughes, Thomas, *A Journal*, Cambridge, England, 1947.

Jackson, Anne, *Early Stages*, Boston, 1979.

Johnson, Harry, and Frederick S. Lightfoot, *Maritime New York in 19th-Century Photographs*, New York, 1980.

Kaplan, Justin, *Walt Whitman*, New York, 1981.

Kasson, John F., *Amusing the Million*, New York, 1978.

Koolhass, Rem, *Delirious New York*, New York, 1978.

Lancaster, Clay, *Old Brooklyn Heights*, Rutland, Vermont, 1961.

———, *Prospect Park Handbook*, New York, 1972.

Landsman, Alter F., *Brownsville*, New York, 1969.

———, *A History of New Lots*, Port Washington, New York, 1977.

Lee, Basil Leo, *Discontent in New York City, 1861–1865*, Washington, D.C., 1943.

Lockwood, Charles, *Bricks & Brownstone*, New York, 1979.

Mack, Gene, *Hall of Fame Cartoons, Major League Ball Parks*, New York, 1950.

McCullough, David, *The Great Bridge*, New York, 1972.

———, *Mornings on Horseback*, New York, 1981.

McCullough, Edo, *Good Old Coney Island*, New York, 1957.

McLoughlin, William G., *The Meaning of Henry Ward Beecher*, New York, 1970.

Ment, David, *The Shaping of a City*, Brooklyn, 1979.

———, and Mary S. Donovan, *The People of Brooklyn*, Brooklyn, 1980.

———, with Anthony Robins & David Framberger, *Building Blocks of Brooklyn*, Brooklyn, 1979.

Miller, Henry, *Book of Friends*, Santa Barbara, California, 1976.

Miller, Rita Seiden, ed., *Brooklyn, USA*, Brooklyn, 1979.

Morris, James, *The Great Port*, New York, 1969.

Murphy, Mary Ellen and Mark, and Ralph Foster Weld, eds., *A Treasury of Brooklyn*, New York, 1949.

Nordoff, Charles, *The Communist Societies of the United States*, New York, 1875.

Pilat, Oliver, and Jo Ranson, *Sodom By the Sea*, New York, 1941.

Postal, Bernard, and Lionel Koppman, *Jewish Landmarks of New York*, New York, 1964.

Reier, Sharon, *The Bridges of New York*, New York, 1977.

Roosevelt, Theodore, *New York*, New York, 1891.

Rosenberg, Charles E., *The Trial of the Assassin Guiteau*, Chicago, 1968.

Rugoff, Milton, *The Beechers*, New York, 1981.

Simon, Donald, *The Public Park Movement in Brooklyn, 1824–1873*, unpublished dissertation, NYU, 1972.

————, "Brooklyn in the Election of 1860," *NYHSQ*, 1967.

Smith, David, *David Smith*, New York, 1968.

Stern, Zelda, *The Complete Guide to Ethnic New York*, New York, 1980.

Stevenson, Elizabeth, *Park Maker, A Life of Frederick Law Olmsted*, New York, 1977.

Stiles, Henry R. *History of the City of Brooklyn*, Brooklyn, Vol. 1, 1867, Vol. II, 1869.

————, *The Civil, Political, Professional and Ecclesiastical History and Commercial and Industrial Record of the County of Kings and the City of Brooklyn, New York*, Brooklyn, 1884.

Swain, Mary B., *Old South Brooklyn Neighborhood Survey*, Brooklyn, 1913.

Talese, Gay, *The Bridge*, New York, 1964.

Thomas, Lately, *The Mayor Who Mastered New York*, New York, 1969.

Trachtenberg, Alan, *Brooklyn Bridge, Fact and Symbol*, New York, 1965.

Vanderbilt, Gertrude, *The Social History of Flatbush*, New York, 1881.

van der Zee, Henri and Barbara, *A Sweet and Alien Land*, New York, 1978.

Ward, William J. and Margaret, "The Green-Wood Cemetery," *JLIH*, 1975.

Warriner, Edwin, *Old Sands Street Church*, New York, 1885.

Weld, Ralph Foster, *Brooklyn is America*, New York, 1950.

————, *Brooklyn Village*, New York, 1938.

White, Norval, and Elliot Willensky, *The AIA Guide to New York City*, New York, 1978.

Whitehouse, Roger, *New York Sunlight and Shadow*, New York, 1974.

Younger, William Lee, *Old Brooklyn in Early Photographs, 1865–1929*, New York, 1978.

About the Author

David W. McCullough, a member of the editorial board of the Book-of-the-Month Club, is the author of *People, Books & Book People* (1981). His work has appeared in *Redbook, Saturday Review, Playboy,* and *The New York Times Book Review*. Born in Canonsburg, Pennsylvania, and raised in Upstate New York, Mr. McCullough is a graduate of the University of Rochester. He lived in Brooklyn for seventeen years and now makes his home in Hastings-on-Hudson, New York, with his wife—a book editor— and their two teenage children.

About the Photographer

Jim Kalett is a free-lance photographer whose work has appeared in *Newsweek, Time,* and *Country Journal*. His first book, *People & Crowds*, was published in 1978. Prior to his free-lance career he was well known in the field as a black-and-white printer, and his lab did darkroom work for nearly all of New York's publishers and many major magazines. Born in New Britain, Connecticut, Mr. Kalett is a graduate of Carnegie-Mellon University. He has lived in Brooklyn for twenty-four years, and currently resides in Park Slope with his wife and son.